B & T

STO

ACPL ITEM
DISCARDED

DO NOT REMOVE
CARDS FROM POCKET

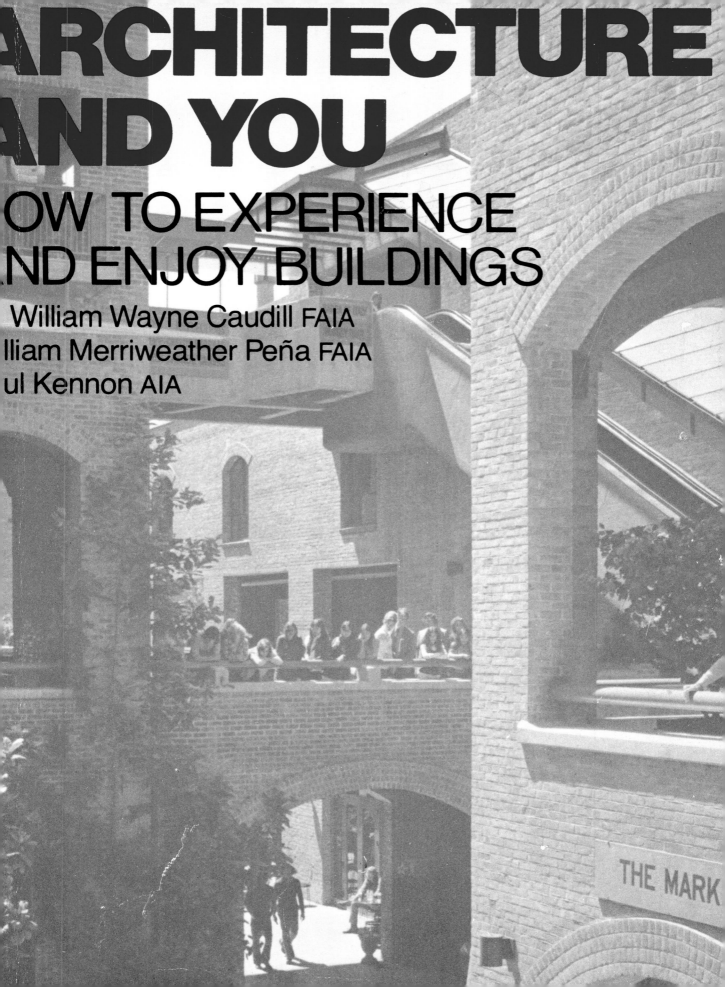

ARCHITECTURE AND YOU

HOW TO EXPERIENCE AND ENJOY BUILDINGS

William Wayne Caudill FAIA
William Merriweather Peña FAIA
Paul Kennon AIA

THE MARK

ARCHITECTURE AND YOU

ARCHITECTURE AND YOU

HOW TO EXPERIENCE AND ENJOY BUILDINGS

By William Wayne Caudill FAIA
William Merriweather Peña FAIA
Paul Kennon AIA

Whitney Library of Design
an imprint of
Watson-Guptill Publications/New York

Frontispiece A well-designed building, like a beautiful painting, a fine piece of sculpture, or a magnificent musical composition, can be a source of enjoyment and inspiration.

Paperback Edition
First Printing, 1981

Copyright © 1978 by Whitney Library of Design

First published 1978 in the United States and Canada by Whitney Library of Design, an imprint of Watson-Guptill Publications, a division of Billboard Publications, Inc., 1515 Broadway, New York, N.Y. 10036

Library of Congress Catalog Card Number: 77-20138
ISBN 0-8230-7040-9
ISBN 0-8230-7041-7 pbk.

ACKNOWLEDGMENTS

CRS Team—Editor: Jan Talbot; Manager: Sandra Baecht; Graphic Designers: Dennis Felix, Joe Van Nest; Librarian: Joy Taylor; Editorial Assistants: Donna Dickinson, Lynn Sitterding.

Contents

7022469

Introduction

What is architecture and how is it perceived? That's what this book is about. We're architects. We have all the biases of architects. We are not architectural historians. Nor architectural critics. Certainly not architectural theologians. We are hard-nosed practitioners, and with our professional associates on the Caudill Rowlett Scott (CRS) team, we have designed hundreds of buildings used by millions of people throughout this country and around the world.

We know about users. We know well their complaints: buildings that get in the way of the things they want to do. Buildings that are too hot or too cold. Buildings that leak. Or crack. Or just get worn out. We also know well users' joy of relaxing, working, learning, buying, manufacturing, and worshipping in buildings which were designed with love and tender care as well as function in mind. We've learned that buildings can be important to the enrichment of life. And after three decades of practice, we are still learning how users interact with space and form and how skillfully designed space and form respond to human needs.

If you want the nuances of esthetic judgment relating to great buildings of all ages or detailed knowledge of specific buildings, you have the wrong book. If you want the philosophies of famous architects, you won't find them here. If you are looking for comparative, evaluative criteria of historical styles, look elsewhere. There's a selected reading list for further study in the back of the book.

If you're looking for a book with the simplicity that experience and knowledge can give, read this one. We hope it's a good teacher of appreciation for everyday buildings.

We're committed to the belief that buildings help people do their jobs or impede them and that good buildings bring joy as well as efficiency.

We think enjoyment of space and form is a birthright. This enjoyment can be heightened in two basic ways: through the thoughtful design of buildings and related spaces and through the user's development of awareness and perception of architecture.

From the beginning of our firm in 1946, CRS was committed to the concept of team practice—designers, technologists, and managers working in concert. We are still striving to perfect team action. One group to whom this book is addressed are the technologists—structural engineers, civil engineers, mechanical engineers, electrical engineers, and technological consultants. We hope that after reading the book they will add a humanist factor to their scientific approach so they can make an even greater contribution to team action. We hope too that managers will find inspiration from the thoughts contained here—particularly the nonarchitects who contribute heavily to successful team action—and that will lead to increased cooperation. Designers can only succeed in their task of creating functional, beautiful space and form if technologists and managers work with them as empathetic partners. We hope this book will help.

But most of all we hope this book will make you more knowledgeable about everyday buildings.

How can you do this? One way is simply to "look and feel." When you see an interesting building, take time to walk around and through it.

Another way is to read. There are hundreds of books—some very good ones—written about buildings and the great historical styles. It's good to know about the conceptual and visual excitement of these masterpieces. There are scores of good books written about great architects. Read them too. Knowing how architects think leads to a better understanding of why buildings are the way they are. Read current articles by architectural critics and historians. The authors of this book, through their experience as architectural practitioners, have encapsulated enough information here to give you the basics of buildings and users' response. Additional reading and regular visits to buildings will also increase knowledge that intensifies the architectural experience.

As you read more about buildings, you'll see words like site, fenestration, the envelope, regionalism, proportion, scale, composition, unity, pattern, texture, light, color, balance, symmetry, asymmetry, shape, rhythm, repetition, solids, voids, mass, and volume that all relate to the physical aspects of buildings. These words have evolved from the time when people decided buildings must be more than mere shelter. You will also run across concepts like timeless quality, human scale, symbolic expression, social context, complexity, and ambiguity. Some are current buzz words which architects like to use, and they are not so difficult to handle if you discard the verbal camouflage and dig for the essence. Understanding them will greatly increase your awareness and subsequent appreciation of space and form.

This book is for laypeople. It's the kind of book we hope architects will like to give their clients. It's a book for students of architecture, families of architects, members of building committees, users of buildings, and anyone else who wishes to improve his or her awareness, perception, and appreciation of buildings.

If architects who read it see their mission in life more clearly, we won't say, "We're not surprised"; just, "We lucked out."

[signatures]

William Peña

1. Appreciation

Two men attend a concert. One
studied music. Has a trained ear.
Spent years developing a high degree of music appreciation. Loves
great works of great composers.
This concert is heaven to him.

To the other man, the concert is a
bore. He has had little exposure to
serious music. No real knowledge of
music. Never learned to listen.
Doesn't even know that he's been
deprived of the pleasure of fine music. He can hardly wait until the concert's over.

A full house at a concert provides an architectural experience as well as a musical experience.

It's intermission. The same two people react very differently as they walk around and within the concert building experiencing its space and form. Now the music lover is bored. He knows almost nothing about buildings. He's visually illiterate. The other person, however, has spent years developing an appreciation of buildings. He has a trained eye. He derives pleasure from the quality of space and form of the great hall. He is stirred to maximum enjoyment. To him, architecture is visual music.

Space, form, and changing light create visual enjoyment.

People who develop appreciation of architectural space and form can experience as much enjoyment as those who have developed appreciation of music.

The term "architecture appreciation" is used here to promote the idea that architecture can be enjoyed, much as the performing or visual arts, physically through the senses.

Architecture appreciation, like music appreciation or art appreciation, is learned. In music, it's learning how to *hear*. In art, how to *see*. In the case of architecture, it's learning how to *perceive*.

If you want to enjoy architecture, there are plenty of opportunities. In your home. In your shopping center. In your place of worship. Wherever people are, there are buildings. Where buildings are, there can be enjoyment.

Enjoying buildings requires some knowledge and some practice in perceiving space and form. Knowledge? Yes, you need to *know* something about buildings: How are they built? How do they help people function? You need to hone your awareness. You need to know something about yourself too. How do you respond to space and form? Zero in on yourself.

You are three in one. You're physical. You're emotional. You're intellectual.

When you come out of a cold, driving rainstorm into the shelter of a warm, dry building, you appreciate that building physically. At the same time, your emotions may come into play. If so, you appreciate the building because you like its color, texture, shape, and size, although you may not know why. Intellectual? You know the "whys."

You may react primarily, but never solely, physically or emotionally or intellectually. Full appreciation is a three-in-one action. When all three—physical, emotional, and intellectual—interact vigorously, the architectural experience promises to reach maximum enjoyment.

PHYSICAL EMOTIONAL INTELLECTUAL

TOTAL PERSON

2. Architecture

People have been careless in defining architecture. One person thinks of architecture as a specific building; another thinks of architecture as all buildings; another considers architecture as a magical additive that somehow raises the quality of a building from banal to excellent; another thinks of architecture as the "spirit of a building"; another says architecture is a style—some kind of sauce that is poured over the building to give it a historical or modern flavor. There's a story about a Miami hotel owner after a hurricane. When asked what damage it did to his hotel, he replied, "It blew off the architecture, but we still have a good building." It must have blown off the sauce.

Here's our definition of architecture:

Architecture is a personal, enjoyable, necessary experience. A person perceives and appreciates space and form from three distinctly different but interrelated attitudes: from the physical, from the emotional, and from the intellectual. The architecture experience evokes a response which fulfills physical, emotional, and intellectual needs, effecting an enjoyable interaction between the person and the building.

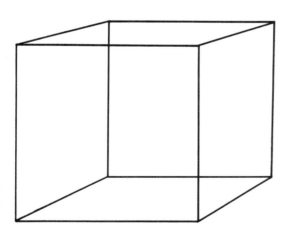  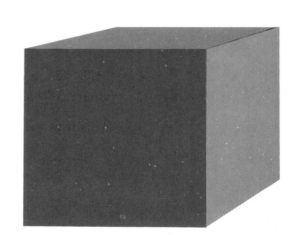

Architecture occurs when a building and a
person like each other.

Stick with this definition. If you wish, remember only the first sentence: Architecture is a personal, enjoyable, necessary experience.

Apply this definition to the following sequence which illustrates the interplay of the physical, emotional, and intellectual. A young woman comes in from the outside where it's hot and humid. She experiences the cool shade and controlled humidity of inside space. Her body says, "I like it." Her physical needs are being met.

The *physical being* takes no notice of proportions, color, texture, furniture, or the painting on the wall.

Then her *emotional being* begins to take over. There is visual awareness. She has a sensuous experience of space and form. "I like the shape of this space. The proportions. I like the color, the texture of the ceiling, the pattern of the floor, the elegant chair, and the colorful painting on the wall."

She likes all these things but doesn't know why. Doesn't care. However, her emotional needs are being fulfilled. Architecture is happening.

Because this young woman knows about buildings—how they are designed, how they affect people—her *intellectual being* responds to the space and form. "What a unique place. The architects knew how to put it all together. And creatively." Intellectually she appreciates (A) the integrated radiant heating in the ceiling and the "clean detailing" where the ceiling joins the walls; (B) the phenomenon of advancing and receding planes created by the vividly colored wall; (C) the exquisitely designed chair by Charles Eames; and (D) the painting that gives visual accent. She likes what she sees and the architectural experience becomes more acute. Knowledge intensifies appreciation.

She has now reached the level where all three factors—the physical, the emotional, and the intellectual—are involved. Architecture has approached maximum intensity and enjoyment.

A simplism? Obviously. Architecture is not that easy to understand. However, on a personal level it's not that complicated either, because you are that person. It's your experience. You know whether you like it or not. You say whether the experience is good or bad. You are the

expert on *you.* If experiencing space and form is enjoyable to you, then architecture happens. It's that simple.

Back to the definition: Architecture is a personal, enjoyable, necessary experience. Why "necessary"?

Just try to escape a building. You are in some kind of a building every day. Whether you realize it or not, buildings do things to you. They exert pressure by being too confining, too open, too hot, too cold, too noisy, too dark, too glaring, not to mention, too dismal. The pressure is real. After 6 or 8 hours in a bad schoolroom trying to learn or in a poorly designed office trying to work, you get edgy. Often because of tension-producing physical environments, people become nervous.

However, a good building, properly designed to respond to human needs, helps the learner to learn, the sick to recover, the worker to work, and the shopper to shop. Great buildings provide more. They stretch human potential through inspiration.

The point is this: buildings are important. They help, or they hinder. And they should foster human advancement—by helping people do the things they need to do. Architecture should make it easier.

You hear people describe buildings as "works of art." That characterization is bad. A building is far more than the personal expression of a designer. In that way, it's not like art. Or music. Although, the design of a good building requires a tremendous amount of artistic ability. Particularly creativity.

Louis I. Kahn, one of the most creative, skilled architects of this century, designed a building (refer to frontispiece) for the University of Pennsylvania that had more influence on architects than any book on architectural philosophy. Following his Richards Medical Research Building was a rash of buildings (plus hundreds of architectural students' projects) which tried to look like Kahn's laboratory. None succeeded. The architects had neither the philosophy, nor skill, nor creativity to match Kahn's work.

Appreciation of the works of creative architects demands creativity on your part. Through accumulated experience and knowledge you design your own appreciation.

Above: The scope of architecture has no limits. You can experience and appreciate an entire city or the smallest detail of a single building.

Good buildings respond to users' needs.

Architecture occurs when you—a creative, knowl-edgeable person—experience an innovative, skillfully designed building.

3. Basics

Consider a few basics on which to build your architecture appreciation.

Your eyes see. Your mind perceives. You look at a brick. You know it's solid. You look at a building. You know it's hollow.

Look at this boxlike cube. Your eyes see *mass.* But your mind perceives *volume.* It's big like a building and buildings are volumetric. You ask, ''What's in this large container?'' You proceed to find out.

You're inside. Contained. You and space. Space defined by form. And you are confined by form. Form which consists of floor, ceiling, and four walls. A building, therefore, is a container of space. And people too.

Experiencing inside space is very different from experiencing the outside. For one thing, it's like being in a box. For another, you get a more intense feeling about inside space. There is no middle ground. You feel either confinement or comfort. Intimidation or stimulation. Restriction or freedom.

The mind perceives a correlation between outside space and form and inside space and form. That's why most architects believe that what you see on the outside of a building should reflect what's on the inside. Their thinking goes something like this: If there is a chimney protruding from the roof, there should be a fireplace attached to it someplace inside—probably the living room or den. Or if there is a wing with beautifully draped windows appropriate for a bedroom, it shouldn't be a garage. The architects are right. A fake chimney insults the intelligence. A garage should look like a garage and not try to fool people into thinking it's a bedroom. A violin looks like it's made for what it does.

You don't have to like the outside to like the inside. But it helps.

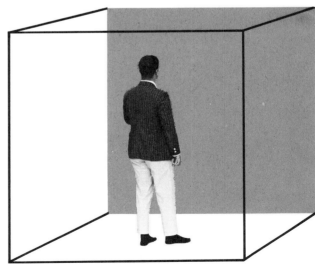

SPACE

A room is a space, although a space isn't necessarily a room. Often a room consists of many spaces, some interlocking and some quite distinguishable.

There are two kinds of architectural space: static and dynamic.

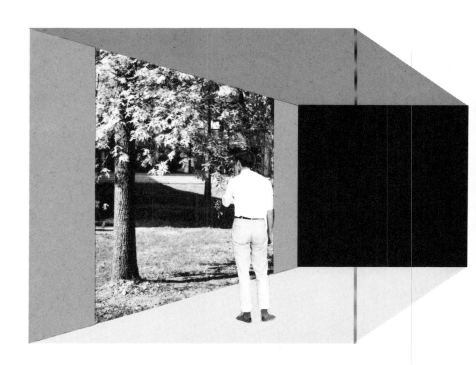

Most people experiencing the Rotunda of the Texas State Capitol in Austin are more aware of the expansive space than the form that confines it, no matter how elaborate that form might be. In many buildings space comes on stronger than form.

It's often said that space is the architect's medium. You go into a building with large volumes, and you will immediately sense its dramatic spatial effects. Sensitivity to space is necessary for architecture appreciation.

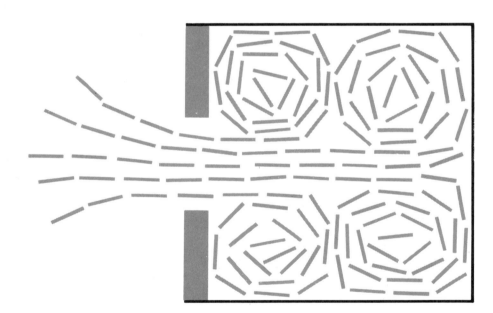

Static space is confined space. No openings. No movement. It's just there. When you close your bedroom at night, drawing the drapes and shutting the doors, you create static space.

Dynamic space is created when you pull the drapes back at dawn to let the new morning into your room. There seems to be a fluid quality about the space. The outside flows in and the inside flows out.

One way to increase your space awareness is to "think, with your eyes." Try to visualize space with floating particles as shown in the diagrams. On the top, space has barriers on four sides. There's no movement. Space behaves like water. When it's damned, it just sits. It's static. Put an opening in the "dam"—a window in the wall, as in the diagram on the bottom—and there's movement. You can't measure the flow, but it's there. Visual dynamics.

When experiencing static space, you may feel that you are inside a box. If you want openness, that inside-a-box feeling is bad. If you want a protective, womblike environment, it's good.

When you experience the visual phenomenon of dynamic space, you may feel that it seems to flow from outside to inside and from inside to outside. The small room appears to be larger than it really is. The feeling of containment is greatly lessened.

It's important to remember that architects design space as well as form. They shape it—give it quality. They can make it flow or jell. They know that two-dimensional floor plans give only the crudest notion of anticipated spatial effects. But even architects sometimes miscalculate. When buildings are first staked out, both client and architect are often fooled by the apparent smallness. Architects know space is a difficult medium. The third dimension causes the most trouble. During the design process, they have to think 3-D. They have to have a highly developed space consciousness. Appreciation too requires thinking in three dimensions. So when you visit an interesting building, think 3-D.

Develop space consciousness.

Some spaces flow. The fluid quality of space
creates visual extension of inside to outside
and outside to inside.

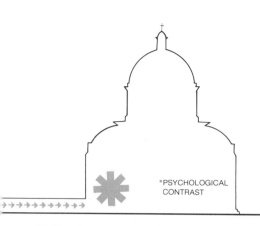

*PSYCHOLOGICAL
CONTRAST

Walking through a low-ceiling, confining area into a high-ceiling, spacious area.

Another way to visualize space and to further develop sensitivity to the myriad spatial effects is to walk through your own home. Observe space discriminately. Note the different sizes and shapes of volumes. Visualize the space of one of the rooms without its walls, ceiling, and floor—as if it were a jelled transparent cube. Visualize the entire dwelling as a system of volumetric cubes. Open a door of a room and observe the volumetric change. The cube joins another cube.

Architects have dealt intuitively with adjoining volumes of space to provide visual pleasure through spatial contrast. Typically, they provide

the experience of walking through a low-ceiling area (the lower, the better) before entering a much larger, higher space. This contrast sufficiently exaggerates the perception of the space change to cause visual shock—at least that first time. Most people love this kind of spatial sequence—the surprise it offers and the relief from monotony.

Learn to identify the kinds of space. Static, dynamic, or combinations. Your home or apartment is an excellent learning laboratory. That's the great thing about architecture appreciation. You don't need to go to a museum or a city auditorium.

FORM

Form is another word of many meanings. It's one thing to the accountant, another to the lawyer, another to the musician, and still another to the athlete. To the architect, form is what you can see in a building. Like a door. A wall. A floor. A ceiling. Overhangs on a roof. Or the whole building. Or the entire city. Form can be of any material—steel, concrete, brick, wood, glass, plastic, or combinations.

Form can have many labels which are confusing. Historians, critics, and architects classify form into categories such as Byzantine, Classical Revival, Gothic, Colonial, Romanesque, Georgian, Tudor, Miesian, Organic, and Modern. Labels like these can be unlimited, particularly if you wish to indulge in the nuances of hybrid styles. Forget the nuances at this point. Stick with the basics.

There are only three basic forms: plastic, skeletal, and planar.

They occur throughout all architecture history. Each of the three basic forms might be rectilinear or curvilinear. If form is rectilinear, its planes or solids are flat—like a square box. If form is curvilinear, its planes or solids are curved—like a round box. Often architects refer to certain forms as "hard" or "soft." They are not referring to the material of the forms, but to their shape. Don't let this confuse you. Soft forms simply do not have very many sharp edges. Hard forms do.

Here are the established characteristics of and differences among the three basic forms.

People love to experience large, public space—inside rooms and outside rooms. They love space that flows.

Opposite page: When you stroll through a building, note its interlocking volumes. Observe too (you may have to use your imagination at first) how form seems to jell space into cubes, partial spheres, cylinders, and other geometric shapes.

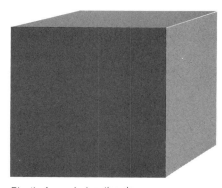

Plastic form during the day

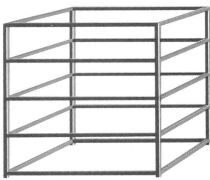

Skeletal form at night

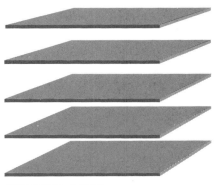

Planar form at night

Plastic. Plastic is sculptural. Note that plastic, as defined here, is not a material. It's a configuration. Think of a building with plastic form as having been sculpted of any material—a mammoth cube of concrete, a huge pile of bricks, or a giant block of wood. Hard, rectilinear plastic forms are cubes, pyramids, and prismatic shapes. Soft, curvilinear plastic forms are domes, spheres, cylinders, and free-form shapes. When you study building configurations, you'll find that most buildings are made up of one or more geometric shapes which give them certain plastic qualities.

Plastic form looks sculptural.

At Harvard University, there is a building designed by CRS which approaches pure plastic form. It looks as if it had been carved out of one huge stone. The building suggests sculpture.

Obviously, a building has to be more than sculpture. It has to work. This one does. Because it does, beauty of form is reinforced by efficiency of function. If this were not a working building, form would be irrelevant—whether skeletal, planar, or plastic.

There was no attempt by the architects to accent the structural

Larsen Hall at Harvard University in Cambridge, Massachusetts, exemplifies distinct plastic form.

frame which holds up the building or to articulate walls and roof planes. Some architects would call this a "skin-covered building." It's more than skin deep. It's a meaningful way of defining plastic form.

Another example of plastic form is Hagia Sophia (Santa Sophia) in Istanbul, Turkey, built around 535 A.D. The total-form (or composite form including all elements of the building), built of half-spheres, cylinders, cones, and cubes, is primarily curvilinear plastic. Isidore and Anthemius, Byzantine architects, outdid Roman architects with daring envelopments of space. The great

interior space created by the large dome is still a marvel. This building epitomizes the perfect marriage of structural engineering with plastic form.

The Hagia Sophia in Istanbul possesses a very strong plastic feeling.

Plastic form has sculptural quality—in mass and detail.

Skeletal. Next consider skeletal form. If you look at any building under construction, you see its structural frame—its skeletal form. The structure is explicit. At a glance, you see what holds up the floors and roof. Columns and beams are distinct.

A ladder is a classic example of skeletal form. So is a saw horse. A greenhouse. An old-fashioned umbrella. Or a Shaker dining room chair. Their bones show.

The columns that seem to race around that ancient and magnificent building—the Parthenon in Athens, Greece—give a skeletal effect. The buttresses of Gothic churches are skeletal. The next time you attend an event in one of the mammoth sports arenas, look at the ceiling and you'll see curvilinear skeletal form. Buildings under construction before the brick or steel panels are in place have beautiful skeletal effects. Architects, observing a building under construction with the steel structure in place, often remark, "It's beautiful now, but wait until the building is walled in. It won't look as good."

Some buildings are designed to retain the skeletal effect. The architects purposely expose the structure, solely for esthetic reasons.

The trained eye experiences much pleasure in seeing structural members actively working—holding up the loads of roofs and floors. Skeletal form derives beauty from its clarity and rationality.

Skeletal form shows its bones.

Crown Hall, at the Institute of Technology (1950–1956) in Chicago, Illinois, designed by Ludwig Mies van der Rohe, is a classic example of rectilinear skeletal form. Bones show. The design features the beams and columns as the important visual elements.

Sit on a chair and you will cause its legs—its columns—to be in compression. Columns usually are. Because columns have tension. But thin columns have a tendency to bend, causing "bending moment." Graceful, slender columns that are designed just right—not too obese, nor too skinny to do the job they're supposed to do—are pleasurable to look at. There is beauty in the logic of economy.

Nature is that way. A rose stem is generally just the right size to hold up a rose. Tree limbs, in a sense, are cantilever "beams." Structure in nature is beautiful because of its economy; so is the building which emphasizes structural members. The members are actually working, holding up "live loads" (people and furniture) and carrying the "dead loads" (building materials). The structural elements are visibly at work.

The Cathedral of Notre Dame in Paris, built around 1200 A.D., is predominantly skeletal form. Gothic architects loved to accent structure, occasionally stretching their virtuosity a bit too far. Some churches tumbled. Most have stood for centuries. What those architects did is rather amazing: stacking relatively small stones (in comparison with the enormous ones used by ancient Egyptians, Greeks, Romans, and Incas) to great heights, enveloping great spaces. Architects today wouldn't dare do this without structural steel or reinforced concrete to serve as a frame on which to secure the stone. But in those days, the stones were the bones. No steel. No reinforced concrete. Innovative Gothic architects, in their ceaseless effort to build upward, invented the buttress to counteract the outward thrust. This evolved into emphatic skeletal form called the "flying buttress."

Crown Hall at the Illinois Institute of Technology in Chicago is a classic example of skeletal form. It displays its structure within a sophisticated system of esthetics.

Flying buttresses of the Cathedral of Notre Dame in Paris are clear examples of skeletal form: visible structural members at work helping to hold up the roof and to keep the walls from falling outward.

Experienced observers of buildings receive much pleasure from the visual clarity of skeletal form.

Planar. Now consider the third basic type—planar form. During the past four decades of the 20th century, a number of buildings have appeared upon the architectural scene, composed primarily of articulated planes—floors, roof, and walls. Architects who designed them were probably influenced by Mies van der Rohe, a master at composing planar as well as skeletal form. Or Frank Lloyd Wright who masterfully used planar form.

Planar form consists of overlapping, sometimes distinct, sometimes interlocking planes—vertical as well as horizontal.

An architect composing planes to achieve total-form might be compared with a person building "a house of cards." This is a ridiculously oversimplified analogy, but it does convey an image of planar form as opposed to plastic and skeletal.

A freestanding partition in a loftlike interior space transmits a strong rectilinear planar effect. So does a freestanding exterior brick wall used as a landscaping element or as a windscreen.

A freestanding serpentine garden brick wall is an example of curvilinear planar form. A horizontal, curved canopy, seen quite often over the automobile entrances of hotels, is another example. Most contemporary buildings have some planar effects.

The German Pavilion at the 1929 International Exposition in Barcelona, Spain, designed by Mies van der Rohe, is a classic example of rectilinear planar form, often called "architecture of planes." Unfortunately, this elegant building, which inspired architects all over the world to work towards purification of form, was demolished—a great loss to everybody, especially the generations of designers to come. Here walls were expressed as freestanding units. Two walls did not make a corner as in most buildings. They were visibly separated, creating a building of articulated vertical planes. Even the roof which rested on the load-bearing walls was expressed as a crisp, separate horizontal plane. Purity of form, distinctness, elegant simplicity made this building one of the most unique in architectural history—one of the first examples of architectural composition which made extensive use of planes.

Vertical planes dominate the composition of the Christian Science Organization Building at the University of Illinois, Urbana, Illinois, designed by Paul Rudolph in 1962. Note how certain planes are notched and grouped to give continuity and visual coherence.

The Barcelona Pavilion, designed by Mies
van der Rohe and built in 1929 at the International Exposition in Spain, established a
new way of composing roof planes, wall
planes, and walking planes.

Paul Rudolph's Christian Science Organization Building is a skillfully designed composition of vertical planes.

Above: Planar form, when composed artistically, can be most impressive, as these photographs show. Note planes are horizontal as well as vertical. Also note the variety. None look alike.

Opposite page: The total-form of Dulles Airport in Washington, D.C., has been masterfully composed. There is a predominant planar effect caused by the "hung roof"; the roof is hung with cables like the Golden Gate Bridge. This permits a relatively thin roof slab. Other forms in this outstanding building, designed by Eero Saarinen, are visually subservient to the giant curvilinear planar roof.

TOTAL-FORM

here are good reasons for learning to recognize these three kinds of form. The process itself teaches awareness. It's a lot easier, and you'll be on more sound ground, if at first you limit your study to the three basic forms. Don't try to classify buildings into the hundreds of styles and quasi-styles that have occurred throughout history. Even architects can't remember the labels. "Texas Cape Cod," however, is one to forget.

Develop an awareness of the myriad forms that compose a building. Their proportions. Their relationships. The spaces they define. How successfully have space and form been composed into an artistic total-form? It's this total-form that registers the strongest impression.

What kind is it? Predominantly plastic form? Skeletal form? Or planar form? Ask yourself too which is best—plastic, skeletal, or planar? You'll find that one is no better than another. Most buildings have all three.

The most artistically successful buildings are those with one predominant form.

It makes no difference which one. All three basic form types have been made into architectural masterpieces by skilled architects. Frank Lloyd Wright and Mies van der Rohe, for example, have designed superb buildings, some of which are predominantly plastic, some predominantly skeletal, and some predominantly planar. Less skillful architects often design buildings which result in nebulous total-form. When a building can't make up its mind what form it is there's visual confusion. Great buildings make clear statements.

Eero Saarinen, architect of the St. Louis arch, was a master at composing complex curvilinear structural elements into strong, simple statements. The Dulles Airport in Washington, D.C., is an example of his great compositional skills, mixed with an uncanny intuition of structural design. The giant curved planar roof dominates.

Not only are the best buildings designed within the limits of one predominant form, but that form type is used consistently throughout the building from mass to smallest detail.

A QUICK REVIEW
A building is composed of space and form. There are two kinds of space: dynamic (space with a fluid effect) and static (space that seems to be boxed in). And three kinds of form: plastic (looks like sculpture), skeletal (shows its bones), and planar (accents planes). All can be counted on one hand.

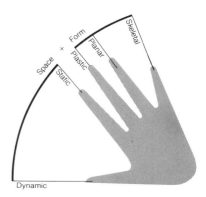

4. Envelope

Architects and engineers generally refer to walls, roofs, and floors of the building as the envelope. Some knowledge of the envelope is needed for optimum architecture appreciation. Let's examine the wall.

WALL

A wall offers visual privacy, true. But a curtain can do that too. Walls do more, depending on whether they are interior walls or exterior walls and what specific functions they have been designed to perform.

There are many kinds of walls which perform many different functions. The two general classifications are interior walls and exterior walls.

Interior. Interior walls are generally lightweight. In conceptual terms, most interior walls are space dividers. These don't have to hold up floors or the roof, so they can be light and just strong enough to support themselves. These usually exist for privacy only—visual, audio, or both. If only audio privacy is required, glass walls can be used more effectively. Half-inch glass stops sound better than most standard residential interior walls. In schools walls also serve as vertical teaching surfaces, holding tackboards, peg boards, chalkboards, and shelving tracks. The Shakers in the last century used walls to hang furniture, equipment, and tools. That's done today too. Furniture (desks, files, book cabinets) is hung on walls. Houses, offices, schools, and some times hospitals use "storage walls" as space dividers.

Some interior walls have to be heavy to function properly. Of necessity vaults, jail cells, and fur storage rooms need to be heavy. Some interior walls must support the roof or the floor above and must be comparatively heavy to be loadbearing.

Opposite page: Think of interior walls as furniture. Most can be moved. Some hold shelves and cabinets and even have desks bracketed from them. Others have chalkboard, tackboard, and builtin screens for slides and movies. Some interior walls are glass to provide audio privacy. And then there are walls hung from the ceiling as space dividers and display surfaces.

Below: A wall is more than a visual screen.

This freestanding wall, which serves as a windbreak, also provides benches for school children.

Exterior. Exterior walls support the roof of a building. They also have two other functions: the outer surface provides shelter from the elements, and the inner lining acts as an interior wall. Exterior walls help maintain the desired interior temperature. They also serve as sound barriers, particularly if the building is adjacent to a busy thoroughfare, airport, outdoor sports facility, or recreation park.

Freestanding outside walls can be designed specifically to create "sun pockets," "wind shadows," and "wind walls" that create venturi effects to temper climate so outside spaces can be used. "Pressure walls" are used to direct cool breezes through windows into leeward areas.

A glass wall is a good device to capture a magnificent view; to make a room look larger; to minimize the demarcation from inside to outside; to permit people on the outside to see the inside, as in an automobile showroom, a newspaper plant, or a soft-drink bottling plant; to provide maximum daylight; and to serve as a windbreak that does not ruin the view of the landscape.

Exterior walls can be of almost any durable material. Each material causes a different emotional response. Try this experiment on yourself. See how you react to the six materials shown here. How do you feel about the brick wall (above left)? Is it hard? Soft? Weak? Strong? Permanent? Temporary? Warm? Cold? Modern? Outdated? Then go to the next wall (above), which is stucco. Ask yourself the same questions. Then try the concrete wall (opposite page, top left). And the steel wall (top right). And the stone wall (bottom left). And finally the glass wall (bottom right). Which wall sent you the most gratifying signals? Try a similar experiment at the sites of different buildings constructed with different materials.

ROOF

One of the most important elements of the envelope is the roof. It does everything from keeping the rain out to keeping the heat in.

Roofs as elements of visual expression have been historically important. During the Middle Ages cathedral roofs dominated town silhouettes, and the thatch roof was particularly prominent on English houses. The mansard roof was a distinguishable feature of 17th-century France. The flat tile roofs of Japan gave unity to an entire neighborhood, as did the slate roofs of Georgian buildings and the curved tiles of Spain and Mexico. Plastered and tiled brick domes and vaults dominated the skylines of the 10th-century Middle East. Today in the U.S. some buildings (including most state capitols) have gold domes to express importance and brighten the skylines.

In the 1850s came the invention of asphalt builtup roofs which played havoc with beautiful sloping and curved roof shapes. As buildings became wider, the sloping roof no longer worked. Can you imagine a one-story building a cityblock wide with a sloping roof? The typical residential slope is approximately 45°. Put the same kind of roof on the cityblock wide building and the peak of the ridge would be at least 13 stories high.

Builtup roofs certainly haven't added charm or visual excitement. Yet ugly as they are, they are with us. What can we do about them? Architects try to hide these eyesores with parapet walls (extensions of exterior walls above the roof line). Some designers use fake mansard roofs to hide the real flat roof—but not successfully. The elimination of the visible roof has reduced the joy of buildings.

Roof patterns and textures enhance the architectural experience.

Not many buildings have two roofs. The top roof keeps the sun off the other one. Hot air collected between the two is carried off by the breeze. Two-roof buildings are nothing new. They were used centuries ago in grass hut villages.

This old mansion (1885) has the famous mansard roof named after architect François Mansart, who wielded great influence in the mid-17th century. Two centuries later in Paris mansard roofs provided a seventh story where only six were allowed by decree. To-day the recent rash of fake mansards have no attic rooms behind them.

Architects like Mies van der Rohe, Le Corbusier, Walter Gropius, and Marcel Breuer did not depend upon the roof to dominate or even enrich the composition. They contended that buildings need no hat—that total-form is stronger without a roof trying to compete in a visual fight with a wall.

A roof is an umbrella, often protecting exterior walls. Like a wall, a roof may also have windows that let light into the inside envelope. And, of course, a roof must try to bounce back the hot rays of the sun.

Most penthouse views from high midtown buildings to the roofscape below show a literal junkyard—unsightly elevator shaft tops, exhaust outlets, plumbing stacks, compressors, air-conditioning units, ductwork, cooling towers, parapet walls with bracings, fire walls, and many square miles of dull asphalt or tar roofs. No visual order whatsoever.

But it needn't be this way. Mechanical elements can be very beautiful in a sculptural way. Architects are beginning to realize that you can't hide a roof. Some now design buildings on the premise that:

The roof is a facade.

Above: In Grand Rapids, Michigan, there is an example of the concept of "the roof is a facade." The roof is a painting by Alexander Calder. Lookdown vistas like this one offer many opportunities for building owners to give their highrise neighbors a visual treat. The owners may own the building, but the neighbors own the view.

Pages 41–42: The technology of this century helped produce just about every kind of roof form imaginable. The variety runs from seemingly no roof to all roof. The roofs shown represent only three basic types. In general, compositions are weak when roofs turn out have the same dominance as walls. In this visual fight one must rule over the other.

FLOOR

Architects often refer to the materials of the envelope as the "fabric."

Think of a floor as walk-on fabric.

You'll be more conscious of materials, colors, patterns, and textures. The notion of walking on a fabric makes one more sensitive to the walking plane. This leads to greater appreciation.

When you walk, you look down more than you may realize. People are more aware of the walking plane than they are of the walls, ceilings, and roofs. Experienced architects know this. They take great care in selecting material and choosing color, texture, and pattern. Thomas Jefferson loved to work with brick as the surface for walks and outside steps. There are original brick steps still in use at the University of Virginia. Both inside and outside brick floors are considered beautiful by most people, if not comfortable for women with spike heels and children on roller skates. Frank Lloyd Wright liked to use native stone for floors. Mies van der Rohe liked machined marble and terrazzo. Wood is still a favorite among architects and home owners despite the advent of low-cost carpeting.

Walking on brick, marble, wood, and carpeting sends different sensuous signals from feet to brain. Some teachers swear that carpeting a classroom minimizes discipline problems. Men walking in a public building from a tile corridor to a carpeted portion have been seen to take off their hats. The sound absorption quality of carpeting may have affected them. During the school building boom in the 50s when wall-to-wall carpets implied lavish spending, architects wouldn't dare call a carpet a carpet. They called it "acoustical flooring."

Floors can contribute to better lighting or they can cause glare. Floors can help or hinder hearing. Sloping floors can improve sight lines. Stepped floors are used as an economical way of designing buildings on sloping sites.

Most people like changes of level. Split-level homes, split-level restaurants, even split-level classrooms have appeal. People like buildings that "ride the contours." The next time you walk into a building for the first time, note your own reaction. Do you look at the floor first? Does the floor feel good? Are there split levels? Do you like the sensation caused by split levels?

Exterior floors—decks, terraces, plazas, and walks—also contribute materially to the architectural experience. It's the walking plane that counts, inside or outside.

Most people love to walk on brick or tile. They get a feeling of time-tested solidity—a good footing, so to speak. Masonry floors imply quality and permanency with their own builtin colors. Patterns and textures are also eye-appealing.

When does a floor stop being a floor? Where is the demarcation when carpets go up the walls? When hospitals use the same hard-surface, germ-resisting, easy-to-clean materials for both floor and wall? Eero Saarinen, in his search for pure plastic form, desired a one-material building. His TWA terminal in New York City (opposite page) certainly comes near his goal. When most people experience this building, they get the feeling that they are walking *in* sculpture.

Richard Neutra used one material for both inside and outside floors, erasing the visual difference between inside and out and strengthening the planar effect in his Tremaine House, in Santa Barbara, California (above). Here the practical and esthetic handling of a flooring material (polished terrazzo) reinforces his architectural statement that outdoors is a part of indoors.

Opposite page: Floors of different levels are almost always appreciated. They break the monotony. They create interesting lookdown and lookup views that most buildings don't have.

Below: When is a wall a window? When is a window a wall? When view is what you are after, either you need a glass wall or a big window. Call this one what you will, the first consideration is the view. This one has it. The second consideration is climate. The sun is not a problem because of the northeast exposure. There are plenty of shade trees. And there is no chilling north winter wind. Put this house in another region, and the glass wall would be illogical. Where it is makes sense.

WINDOWS

Most envelopes have windows. Don't take the simple window for granted. It's quite an invention. Windows are the eyes of the envelope, and more. The words "fenestration" and "window" are used interchangeably by architects. Fenestration simply means the design, arrangement, and proportions of window groups.

Windows have three basic functions: (1) to admit natural light, (2) to admit and emit air, and (3) to afford a view.

Common window types such as casement, sliding, projected, center pivoted, louvered, and double-hung are designed to perform all three tasks.

Some windows, however, are designed to do only one task. The prime function of clerestory windows, windows of saw-tooth construction, and skylights (horizontal windows) is to admit light from the sky.

Windows have three basic tasks: To provide lighting (top); to provide ventilation (middle); and to provide view (bottom). Most windows try to do all three, but aren't successful. Often there's too much compromise. These specialized windows work better.

Every window should have a function.

Opposite page: In the 50s architects seemed to discover the "ribbon window." Actually ribbon windows were used much earlier by Wright and Le Corbusier, but in the 50s their use spread throughout the U.S. (top left). The "punched hole window" was taboo. A few years later the ribbon window literally ate up the wall. Walls became glass; the "window wall" arrived (top right). It was the in thing, although Mies was using window walls before the 30s. During the 60s, probably because of boredom rather than lifestyle changes or technological advances, architects rediscovered the "punched hole window." It prevailed for nearly a decade (bottom left). And what did those magnificent, but slightly erratic architects do next? They rediscovered the ribbon window (bottom right).

Some windows are designed to serve only as "wind windows"—permitting air to flow through a building. The apex of the wigwam that serves as an efficient exhaust is a wind window. The *malkaf* of the Islamic houses built in the 17th century is an ingenious device which scoops the wind from the roof and lets it flow into deep interior space. In the U.S. during the 50s, before air-conditioning, architects innovated many ways of putting the wind to work. They used wind baffles to guide gentle breezes to the "living zone" near the floor, louvers to direct too-strong winds over people's heads, and openings in interior partitions to allow breezes to flow from one room to another. (Some such interior windows also filter out extraneous sound.) These glassless windows that only admit a breeze do a good job of providing comfort in hot, humid regions.

And, there is the view window, dubbed by homebuilders the "picture window." When it's located on the street side, there is always the question: What or who is the picture—the street or you? Unfortunately, view works both ways unless it's one-way glass—and that reverses at night.

The window that provides a view is best if it is without screens (the ventilation requirement should be provided elsewhere) and without restrictive sun control such as a grill. Who wants a "grilled view"?

If you want to have some fun, try to perceive certain window groupings as musical expression. With a little imagination you can see some beating a 1–1–1 rhythm; others a 1–2, 1–2 rhythm; others playing a waltz in 3-quarter time and some in 4–4 time. You might even envision ribbon windows as hold notes. If you look hard enough, you might even see syncopation. (Some facades, for example, that on Harvard's Larsen Hall on page 22, carry a pronounced syncopation effect.)

Know how a window works; then you can appreciate it. Buildings and building components must work. They just can't sit there.

1-1-1

1-2   1-2

Waltz

4-4 time

Rhythm in windows

The outside wall doesn't own the window. Architects decided that since the window was such a great invention, it should be used on the inside too. The window is a fine device to create dynamic space, to eliminate feelings of confinement, and to provide interesting lookup and lookdown views in multistory buildings.

Throughout this book you read the expression "space and form" many times. Note "space" always comes first. Architects think "space" first these days. Fifty years ago, their first concern was with form, generally the facade. Today architects, through design, seek to create interesting spatial effects. Form comes second because form defines space. Good reasons for this.

Architects found empirically, rather than through research, that floors, even more than cell-like rooms, foster social divisiveness and

isolation. So they opened up the inside of their buildings vertically as well as horizontally. They eliminated big chunks of walls and floors from their plans. They provided interior windows; some with panes, some without. Their buildings became more socially oriented and less like eggcrates. Amenities resulted with no extra cost to owners. A good move.

There was another benefit. The energy crunch suggested keeping outside windows to a minimum. But when outside vistas are eliminated, so are certain amenities. Therefore the challenge to the architect was to create inside vistas as interesting as outside vistas. They did, as some of these photos show. One architect aptly put it, "We took the windows from the outside walls and put them in the inside."

STRUCTURE

Something must hold up the floors, the roof, and the walls. That's the structure.

How much should you know about structural technology to fully appreciate a building? Obviously not as much as a structural engineer, a mechanical engineer, an electrical engineer, or a civil engineer, each of whom plays a major role in the design process. It would be a distraction if you knew all about tension and compression stresses of beams, girders, and columns; about heat flow and air distribution; about electrical distributions and overloads; and about nuances of water and waste disposal—however glamorous they might be to engineers. So continue to stick with the basics. Since a building's structure is often visible, some knowledge of structure is advisable. This one-paragraph history may help.

Structure spans space. Ancient Egyptians used large stones (A). The *beam* came into being. Spans were limited to the sizes of the stones which could be found and lifted into place. Centuries later some one discovered how to span larger spaces with smaller stones (B). The *arch* was invented, which led to the vault, which led to the dome. Arch technology reached its height during the era of the great Gothic churches. About the same time, someone else discovered that you could take short sticks of lumber, tie them together in triangular arrangements, and span even larger spaces (C). The *truss* was invented. The battle of capturing even larger volumes of space requiring greater spans continued until this century when structural engineers perfected cable suspension structures (D). *Suspension structures*, such as the Golden Gate Bridge which represents the advanced technology of this age, came into being. The suspension building arrived. Next may be the spanning of entire cities. The latest innovation is encapsulating space (E). *Air structures* are capable of spanning great spaces economically. Like balloons, air pressure holds up the roof.

Technology helps to provide the structural logic of form.

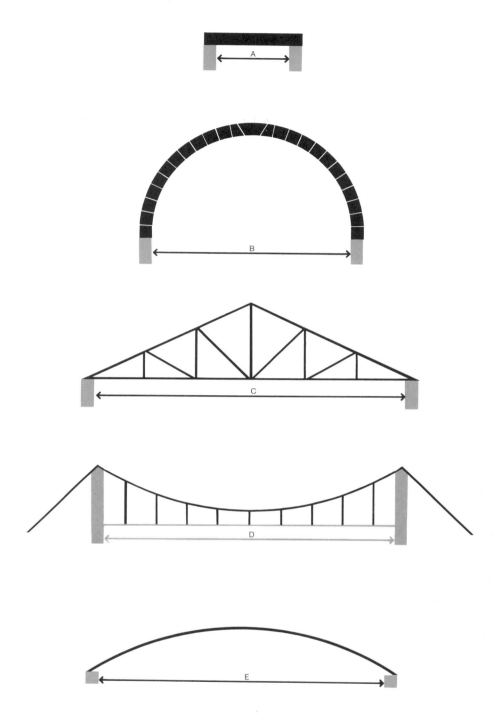

One of the first successful applications of suspended structure applied to a building is Yale University's hockey rink in New Haven, Connecticut (right), designed by Eero Saarinen. Expertly engineered and artistically designed, this building is evidence that sports arenas can be beautiful as well as big. The logic of structure enhances its beauty. A more recent suspended structure is Minneapolis's Federal Reserve Bank (below), designed by Gunnar Birkerts (who had worked for Saarinen). Its lower floors are suspended from cables. The main cable is expressed, creating an interesting facade.

Throughout history, architects have been inspired by new ways to span space. That's why advanced technology intrigues them. Architects practice on the shoreline where two worlds overlap—where science/engineering overlaps arts/humanities.

Opposite page: These two old churches, St. James Episcopal Church in La Grange, Texas (top), built in 1885, and the Christian Science Church in Berkeley, California (bottom), built in 1910, have their structures accented each in its own way. Both are beautiful. Both communicate. One in strong, simple terms. The other in a rich, embellished manner. Each speaks of structure.

Architects are more intuitive than analytical when it comes to structural design. They love and readily accept structural innovations. Fortunately, there are excellent structural engineers to back them up. But it wasn't always that way. There was no solid theory until the last hundred years. What the Egyptians learned was lost. The Romans received only a portion of what the Greeks learned. Renaissance architects wanted nothing to do with Gothic knowledge, which surely would pollute the pure classical. Victorians were copycats without knowing why. Only contemporary architects have had the opportunity to explore structures through scientific methods. And they did. Now the design of structures is based on accurate calculations.

From new theories and new materials new forms emerged.

An exciting, most promising advancement in structure is based on the concept of air pressure holding up a roof. First, "balloon framing" caused a revolution in American wood-frame construction. Around 1840, the introduction of standard sizes in milled lumber and machine-made nails lead to a whole new system of contruction. Now, "balloon structures" may revolutionize the design profession.

Only a few years ago, air-supported structures were looked upon as having no value other than sheltering tomato plants or covering small backyard swimming pools. But encapsulating space was first seriously considered back in 1946 when architect William H. Tuntke proposed an air-supported structure for St. Louis's open-air opera. It wasn't built. Like most ideas, this one required many years before it was translated into concrete form. But then came Expo '70, the World's Fair in Osaka, Japan. Several "innovative inflatables" were built. The most significant was the U.S. Pavilion. With minimum budget and maximum guts and creativity, American designers produced an impressive structure.

The August, 1970 *Progressive Architecture* predicted: "Just as the Crystal Palace awakened Victorians to undreamt of new possibilities of construction in the 1850s, this building (the U.S. Pavilion), with the

Right: One of the most significant buildings of Expo '70, the world's fair held in Osaka, Japan, was the U.S. Pavilion. It was almost a nonbuilding, as this view indicates, but when experienced from the inside, it created a new, unique kind of grand space.

Below: Advanced technology has given architects a brand new structure type—the air structure. Air structures have unlimited possibilities—the larger they are, the more efficient they become. If you can put a building and a park under a bubble, you can put a whole city under one. Buckminster Fuller predicted this years ago with his geodesic domes, but an air structure may actually be the first to envelop a city. But when this happens, will there be buildings as we know them now?

argest and lightest clear-span air-supported roof ever built, may prove to be the most important advance in building technology of the 1970s.'' It has.

Credited as being one of the first large, *permanent* air-supported structures is the Thomas A. Leavy Activities Center at the University of Santa Clara, California, built by CRS five years after Expo '70. Covering 2½ acres, the structure's fabric roof is of tetrafluoroethylene-coated fiberglass. Only five pounds of air pressure per square foot keep the balloon inflated.

Since plants grow in the new environment, the Santa Clara air-supported envelope contains both a building and a park. Visitors who come from all parts of the country to see this building are surprised by the ambience. One remarked, ''I have the funniest feeling. I can't tell whether I am on the inside or the outside.'' This is what intrigues architects—the new quality of space.

Many other exciting structural advancements are in the offing. Significant research in wood, steel, concrete, glass, and plastic continues with the promise of new, more economical and efficient forms.

MATERIALS

The envelope can be made of all kinds of building materials—brick, stone, concrete, wood, glass, steel, plastic; the list goes on. Architects have been known to complain because there are too many. In any case there is a certain propriety in the choice of materials.

Wood is wood. It's not a wallboard made of sugar cane with a photograph of wood on it.

Brick is brick. It's not wallpaper that looks like brick.

Stone is stone. It's not stucco made to look like stone.

Concrete is concrete. It's neither brick nor stone, even if it's scored to resemble them. Each material has its own generic quality relating to structure and texture.

There's nothing wrong with wallpaper, or stucco, or wallboard. Good materials—if used with propriety. But they should be what they are. And they should possess honesty and be reasonably permanent. Like a person, a building has its own integrity. It's not a make-believe stage set. A wood building should not look like stone, as in the case of Mount Vernon. George Washington must have known that.

You don't have to follow the generally accepted rules of texture, color, and form: wood is warm; steel is cold; marble is formal; field stone is informal; shingles are homey; metal roofs are institutional. It's not necessarily true that reds and yellows are warm colors; blues and greens are cool colors. Don't let it worry you if a curvilinear hard steel form looks soft. You be your own judge.

It's a great sport these days for architects and critics to vilify the famous designers of the Modern Movement—Le Corbusier, Mies, Wright, Gropius. Gnats biting the elephants. ''Those guys are too antiseptic. Their buildings are too cold,'' people say. Who has the final word?

Mies's fans would never concede that his steel, glass, and brick houses are cold. They find them vital and therefore warm.

What's warm? What's cold? The architects of Pima College in Tucson, Arizona, were most anxious for the college to have the color and texture of the surrounding desert.

They went to great lengths to specify the exact color and size aggregate so the concrete would match the texture and warm hues of the desert. The results were gratifying. They were delighted with the warm concrete—just like natural stone. Unfortunately for reasons of function and economy, cold-feeling steel panels had to be used for walls along some of the peripheral corridors. Two years after the students moved in, the architects conducted a survey to see what the students thought of their college facilities. Much to the surprise of the architects, the students considered the concrete cold and the steel panels warm. Maybe the students developed ''Detroit esthetics'' because of the high value they placed on automobiles.

Each material has inherent properties.

Architects must respect these properties. Brick, for example, is strong in compression, weak in tension. Accordingly, bricks make good load-bearing walls and columns; they are excellent for arches; but they make poor beams. However, concrete makes excellent beams. Reinforced concrete has great strength in compression, tension, and bending (beams have to bend), but it doesn't have the builtin color and pleasing texture that bricks have. Bricks and concrete have a tendency to absorb water, so they make poor roofs. Shingles do a better job of repelling water, so they make good roofs. Walls too.

Some architects feel shingles are a bit shaggy or rustic, preferring a more industrialized look. Others feel that brick is archaic and expensive. They argue that every square foot of a 12-inch (30-cm) wall requires about 20 bricks—and each one must be put in place by a mason whose hourly pay is skyhigh. Brick, concrete, and shingles are all good materials and can be economical if used correctly, that is, according to the nature of the specific material. This applies to any material. All are competitive. Most are on the architect's ''palette.'' Some architects prefer to work predominantly with only one material, usually because of esthetics, geography, economy, and availability of skilled labor.

Pages 58-60: A brick building
should have a generic quality—
it should look brick. A concrete building
should look concrete. A wood building
should look wood.

THE MARKET

CONNECTIONS

There are literally millions of connections in most large envelopes. These are called "details." Design excellence depends largely on the care that architects give to the details—like how the walls connect with the floor, how the ceiling joins the walls, and how openings are placed in walls. "God is in the details," said Mies, referring to the love and tender care given to the small connections.

Superb buildings have superb details.

Highly skilled designers give as much thought to designing a simple window as they do to developing floor plans. They seek "clean" connections.

Some details are disarmingly simple. But quite often it is more expensive to achieve visual economy than it is to cover up a poor connection with the clutter of molding. A drafting room term called "zero detailing" refers to the way glass is joined to concrete, brick, or wood without any visible molding. Zero detailing is important to obtain pure planar form effects, such as that of an inside wall extending to the outside.

Renaissance architects were as much concerned with moldings that joined ceiling to walls and walls to floor as they were with the walls themselves. Unlike contemporary architects, they did not prefer clean connections. Too plain for them. They relished the nuances of modulation between the vertical and the horizontal. It was the style of the day to use moldings as decorative form. Their buildings had a rich elaborate consistency about them. The profiles of the interior base molding (the connection at floor and wall) were miniature versions of the ground connections where exterior walls connected with the ground.

Elegant contemporary buildings do have consistency of mass to detail. The detailing matches the form of the building. For example, planar total-form has planar details. When you experience a building, look at its details closely. You'll find some connections are artfully done; others are botched. The connections you'll examine either consciously or subconsciously are probably those where the building meets the ground and

Ground connection

Sky connection

Generally moldings are used to hide poor connections. Architects abhor the bad workmanship that requires moldings which create "dirty" connections; they like "clean" connections. Frank Lloyd Wright used a technique of installing glass in a stone, brick, or concrete wall with no visible molding—an excellent way to obtain maximum planar effect. Here is an example of "zero detailing" which connects glass to concrete without using molding. Under certain lighting conditions it's hard to tell whether you are inside or outside.

where it meets the sky. A quick look at the sky silhouette will help you determine the character of total-form.

The genius of the Skidmore Owings Merrill (SOM) team, which has designed some magnificent skyscrapers, is found in ground connections. From the fifth floor up, SOM-designed buildings are not unlike other buildings. The difference is the innovative, polished manner in which the buildings stand on their sites.

The problem of ground connection is difficult, even on a flat site. Have you ever seen a house that looks as if it is sinking or has sunk into the soft lawn? Or have you noticed that some houses sit in bushes like birds nesting? Study ground connections on your way home today. A building without some kind of carefully designed base sinks visually. That's why platforms and

berms are used so extensively. The building needs something to sit on.

Many of Le Corbusier's buildings were deliberately designed to "float" above the ground. Corbu's ground connection is the lack of a connection.

Wright felt quite differently about his commitment to earth-and-building separation. He contended that earth and building should be one, with the building literally and physically growing out of the ground. Both architects successfully designed beautiful ground connections. It's not what is done; it's *how* it's done.

Study the connections. You'll learn much about buildings.

The sky connection is the juncture of building and sky. Or it's the outline of the building against the background of sky. The sky connection terminates the building. Architects continually argue how best to terminate buildings. Some insist on doing it with a crisp cutoff, like a large parapet wall to "hide the junk"—elevator penthouses, ventilation shafts, air conditioning appendages, and fire-stair roof exits. Others argue that these should be expressed articulately. They say, "The top floor shouldn't be cut off like a piece of sliced baloney." Some even insist that every building should have a crown, like most state capitols—a hat. No matter what, the sky connection more than any reveals the overt character of the building. The next time you are downtown look at the sky connections. Decide which ones you like the best and why.

ges 64–65: The ground connection—
ere the building meets the ground—is tell-
evidence of the architect's design ability
much as anything else. Wright was a pure
ius at having his residences literally grow
of the earth. Corbusier put a house on
s, completely divorcing the building from

its site. SOM used a variety of techniques,
from setting buildings in water to putting them
on platforms. It's not so much what architects
do with the ground connection; it's how well
they do it. The ground connections of these
buildings were done well.

Pages 66–69: Excellent buildings have excellent details. Sometimes there is as much pleasure in appreciating the details of certain buildings as there is in appreciating the main outlines of the buildings or their spaces. Take a close look at these details. Most have a certain refinement that delights the mind as well as the eye.

Most people want the genuine article, like the old Victorian houses that somehow escaped becoming parking lots. There's a great difference between these wonderful old arks and the new ''old'' houses covered with tasteless icing of a vague, historical flavor. Pure sham. The Victorian houses, as contrived as they were, are real—portraying in a clear language the lifestyle of their day. This is not true of the phony ''styles'' advertised in your Sunday newspaper supplement.

Try to understand great historical buildings. It is of primary importance to be able to identify the three basic forms and the two kinds of space which are common to all buildings. All it takes is practice. You can do it wherever you are by visiting old and new buildings. Remember, most great buildings were very innovative and very modern in their day. Don't be fooled, however, by poor imitations.

The paste-on-front townhouses shown here are not examples of historical styles. At best, they are only caricatures painted on flat facades. They are poor, distorted imitations. The dormers are fake. The shutters don't shut. The balconies are too small for people. The bay windows don't protrude. The half-timbers are not heavy timber, but thin boards with no more structural strength than a coat of paint. No better than billboards with pictures of old styles.

Stage sets. Make-believes. There's lot of kidding going on. The building fooling the users and possibly the users fooling themselves.

These townhouses tell lies. But they don't have to. Today, architect have unlimited opportunities to provide people with beautiful, logical dwellings that are individualized. If "beauty is truth," these houses are ugly because they lie. No logic to form. Unreal "styles" that try to foo people. Imitation denies architecture. On a sophisticated plane imitation kills architecture.

Knowing reasons for historical styles, becoming intimately acquainted with buildings that are rep resentative of those styles, learning about architects who designed buildings during those periods of history—this kind of knowledge helps you appreciate historical buildings as well as the masterpieces of this century.

Old English (?)

Texas Georgian (?)

New Orleans French (?

Classic Modern (?)   Gulf Coast Spanish (?)   Mississippi Colonial (?)

Example: Mr. A and Mr. B visit a 16th-century building designed by Andrea Palladio. It doesn't lie. It's real. It was real 400 years ago. It is real today. Both seem to like it.

Mr. A never heard of Palladio. He just likes the building; he doesn't know why. The building appeals to him emotionally. His architectural experience is limited by his lack of knowledge of buildings and his inability to analyze space and form. His experiencing the building is no big event—just another building he likes.

It's another story for Mr. B. To him, it's pure joy to experience the building. He knows of Palladio's great contribution and influence throughout history. He appreciates Palladio's flawless precision. His principles of scale. Of proportion. Of composition. Of skeletal form. He holds in high esteem the manner of the structural system—the way the roof and floor loads are transferred from arches to columns to arches. He loves the play of spaces. He admires the exquisite materials. Mr. B is stirred intellectually. Knowledge has paid off in extreme pleasure. Architecture comes on strong.

Mr. B has another advantage. Because he knows the history of buildings, he's in a much better position to appreciate the building where he works. With his background, Mr. B can more fully appreciate other fine buildings within walking distance of his office like the community theatre and the concert hall. There are superb buildings in every city for you to enjoy. Increased knowledge intensifies appreciation of excellent buildings. The more you know, the greater your joy.

Recall the definition from the beginning of Chapter 2:

Architecture is a personal, enjoyable, necessary experience.

Houston's twin-tower Pennzoil Building rises over the Civic Center. Jones Hall for the Performing Arts (left) and the Albert Thomas Convention Center (right) form the setting to give this sculpturelike office building a feeling of magnificent grandeur.

PROPORTION

When you experience a building, study its proportion—the relation of one part to another and to the whole. What is the most satisfying proportion? The Greeks thought they knew. Their temples were designed according to certain rules relating to "the golden section." In the 13th century, Fibonnaci put it all down on paper. He said "the golden section" or perfect proportion was .618034 to 1 (about 5 to 8). The Parthenon (including its pediment) fits into this rectangle. So do the pyramids at Giza. In the 16th century, Leonardo Da Vinci wrote a book on geometric recreations called *De Devina Proportione*. In 1948 Le Corbusier wrote a book on mathematical proportioning. Throughout the ages, architects have searched for the golden rule of proportion. They are still searching.

Today we have not only a different way of looking at things, but different things to look at.

The Greek rules of proportion based on stone construction don't apply anymore.

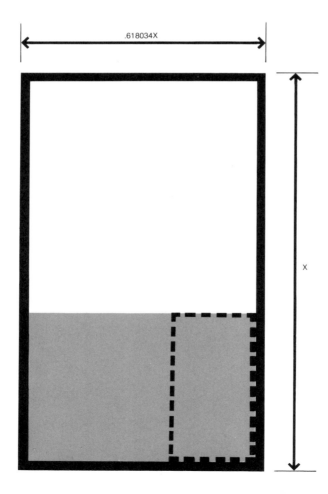

Recent engineering advancements in prestressed and post-tension concrete, together with progress in the metallurgy of steel and aluminum, have made obsolete the always acceptable hand-me-down esthetics of stone. Structural stone is rarely used today, and for good reason. Reinforced concrete is stronger. So is structural steel.

A knowledgeable person finds a concrete column ridiculously obese if it has the same proportions (width to height) as a stone column. He knows that a slender steel column outworks any stone column. Both concrete and steel are more efficient. They cost less too.

What is the most eye-pleasing proportion for a building's structure? Mathematics won't tell you. Proportion must be generically correct. It's one thing for stone, another for concrete, something else for steel.

An ancient Greek Rip Van Winkle viewing the scene today, would be shocked and dismayed to see those steel and concrete buildings which appear to defy gravity. To him, an opening was determined by the size of a stone lintel which rested on two columns. Spanning 10 feet (3 m) was an accomplishment in those days. Today a 60-foot (18-m) span is nothing to get excited about (see the section on Structure in Chapter 4). Obviously when technology permits greater spans with smaller columns and beams, the proportion of solids to voids changes too.

Present technology gives architects and engineers unlimited range to compose new forms and exciting spaces. The esthetics of stone is still correct—for stone. But concrete buildings should look like concrete buildings. That's the basis for an esthetics of concrete. And steel buildings should look like steel buildings—the basis for an esthetics of steel. Steel shouldn't look like concrete; concrete shouldn't look like stone. Proportion differs.

Knowing something about the properties of different materials deepens the appreciation of architecture. It helps even more when you begin to understand why certain materials were chosen.

Architects don't want to admit it, but painters and sculptors have always influenced them. Understandable. In particular, the geometric abstract Dutch painter, Piet Mondrian, had noticeable influence on contemporary architects. There are traces of Mondrian's proportions and colors on many fine buildings.

These two beautifully proportioned houses, whether they were consciously designed as such or not, have strong Mondrian patterns and proportions. The two superb architects who were responsible for these pacesetting residences—Charles Eames, top, and Ralph Anderson, bottom—have completely different personal styles. Each is a master at composing architectural form but in very different ways. Each has a different philosophy of design. Each has a different system of esthetics: "machine esthetics" (top) "structural wood" (bottom). Yet both have design skills together with the creativity to produce masterful architectural compositions. Their skills relate considerably to their ability to produce pleasing proportions.

SCALE

The meaning of scale is elusive. Architects love the ambiguity that surrounds the word. There is more confusion associated with the meaning of scale than with the word "architecture." Here are a few of the expressions used at architects' conventions, in drafting rooms, at competition juries, at seminars, and in critical writing on architecture: human scale, inhuman scale, intimate scale, esthetic scale, small scale, large scale, grand scale, super scale, structural scale, pedestrian scale, automobile scale, residential scale, urban scale, elegant scale, and out-of-scale. That last one is the favorite. Each has different inflections and two or three different meanings. This makes for poor communication, if nothing else.

Don't let this confusion among the professionals bother you. All they are talking about is the relative size of things. If they were more precise, they would say, "This building is twice as big as it should be," or "The ceiling is three times the height of a person when it should be just twice as high," or "The door is 4 feet higher and 1 foot wider than most doors," or "This room is so big I feel like an ant," or "It's so small I feel like a giant." Instead, they say, "It's inhuman in scale," or "It's out of scale."

You are probably thinking: Wouldn't two expressions suffice—too large and too small? It's not quite that simple either. Why is it too large or too small. Ask why, and you'll get a lot of different answers. That's why architects use so many expressions related to the relative size of things.

Don't try to remember and understand every architect's, critic's, or historian's favorite expression relating to scale.

Remember these three terms: physical scale, associative scale, and effectual scale.

It's a good bet that every other kind will fall under one of these headings.

Physical Scale. Physical scale is something you can measure with a yardstick. Stairs, for example. Are the risers 4 inches (10.2 cm) or 7 inches (17.8 cm)? Are they too steep? Are the treads 12 inches (30.5 cm)? Are they wide enough? Is it easy to walk up and down the steps? Is the door wide enough? Can you get a piano through it? Is it large enough for groups to exit through? Or is it just big enough for the cat to use? Is a wall high enough to hang an 8-foot (2.4-m) square tapestry? Is the dining room large enough to seat 12 people? Is a convention center large enough to take care of 4,000 people? Each question refers to physical scale.

When someone implies something is too small by remarking, "It's out of scale," we have a pretty good idea what he means. But if he were more to the point and said, "It's too small to get a piano through," then we know precisely what he is talking about. The physical scale is wrong. It's too small. It doesn't just *seem* too small. It *is* too small physically.

Physical scale is measurable.

eft: Study these two buildings. Note each is redominantly skeletal form. Yet each has a ifferent character primarily because the ructural bays and structural members eams and columns) have much different roportions. And rightly so. One gets its proortions from structural engineering related concrete. The other from structural engieering related to steel. The one should look ke a concrete building; the other a steel uilding. Proportion is determined by the naure of the material.

their search for pleasing proportions, arhitects are deeply concerned with length, idth, and height of interior and exterior volme. They are particularly sensitive to proortions of solids (walls) and voids (windows) nd the relation of height to width of windows. rchitects know that if proportions have a ertain rightness, public acceptance of the ntire building is generally assured.

Associative Scale. Associative scale is difficult to measure. A yardstick won't do. It's one of those "it seems" things. But to the senses it's real and measurable. Your eyes and memory do the measuring.

Try this exercise for understanding associative scale: A person who has seen the Parthenon retains an everlasting image. He is amazed by the giant-size steps built for the goddess Minerva; they're certainly not for humans. He notes the beautiful proportions and the superb workmanship, but he's particularly cognizant of the impressive size of this ancient Greek temple. It's the physical scale of the building that sticks in his mind. Now if this same person were to see another Parthenon with exactly the same proportions, the same material, the same quality of workmanship, the same setting, but only half the size of the original—a different physical scale—his experience would be drastically different. "This is no Parthenon. This is an imitation, a mere miniature of the real thing. What I see is a bad copy." It's bad to him because he associated it with the real thing where the size is so important. Associative scale comes into play. Seeing a miniature, scaled-down version of this grand building is repugnant. Wouldn't you react the same way?

If the person had never seen the original Parthenon, he might have liked the half-size version. If you've never seen a stately or three-story Colonial mansion, the scaled-down one-story versions found in most suburbs are not so bad. If you have seen the real thing, then the miniatures seem like imitations.

A woman living on the outskirts of Houston reported to the sheriff's office that a plane had crashed a mile from her house. Immediately emergency vehicles were dispatched to the scene. What they found was not a terrible wreck—only a slightly bent model airplane 75 yards (70 m) from her house.

It's easy to understand why the woman reported the crash. Her eye deceived her, but only on one item—the physical scale. The plane she saw had exactly the same shapes, the same proportions, the same markings as the real thing. It behaved in the air like the real thing. Associative scale came into play—but it was very real to her.

Associative scale is determined by precedent.

he Greeks probably started it all—using the
column module'' as a basis for proportion-
ng buildings. Later Palladio picked it up.
When small columns were used, everything
lse was small. Today's architects follow no
uch rules which originally applied to stone.
Nevertheless, architects have a keen aware-
ess of the proportions and the visual impact
f columns.

Effectual Scale. A building can be big enough to do its job (satisfying the physical scale); its size can be historically correct (satisfying the associative scale); but what about the psychological aspect of size? How big or how small does the building feel?

Consider the example shown below. The diagram on the left shows a windowless space. It ''feels'' small. Put glass on one side, as illustrated in the diagram on the right, and it ''feels'' much larger, although physically it isn't. But the feeling is real, as real as if it were 3 feet (.9 m) wider and higher. Space has been expanded visually. Now the outside is part of the inside. Effectual scale concerns the illusion of size.

During the late 40s and early 50s, due to material shortages, tight money for building, and strict construction budgets, architects kept floor areas of dwellings to an absolute minimum. Some excellent small houses were built through skillful use of effectual scale. One design technique was to eliminate partitions between such rooms as living, dining, and kitchen areas, making them ''functional areas'' instead of rooms. Had they been rooms with four walls, they would have been unbearably small.

But during this period, houses were built that didn't feel small. Sometimes kitchens would be only feet (1.8 m) wide, with a countertop on one side and the refrigerator, stove, and sink on the other. This le an aisle barely large enough for two people to pass through. Yet, the kitchens had a spacious feeling. Continuous glass was used the length of the kitchen above the countertop and extended to the ceiling. What could have been tunnel-like space turned out to be a delightful, seemingly large kitchen—a case of borrowing the outside to make the inside look larger.

Effectual scale is a little harder to understand when it relates to space and form that seem too large. Consider the top illustration on the opposite page. A man is intimidated by the physical scale of a room. To him something is wrong with the space. The room simply ''feels'' too big to him. The space is overpowering. The ceiling seems too high. The room is too wide for comfort. The man is dehumanized. So he might say, ''The room has no human scale,'' and not be far wrong He feels like an ant in an empty breadbox—lost and insignificant.

''Human scale''? Does it mean 8-foot (2.4-m) ceilings or 80-foot (24 m) ceilings? Does it mean 4-inch (10.2-cm) stair risers or 2-foot (.61-m) risers? Is the scale measurable b a yardstick (or meter stick) or through psychological testing? The concern here is the room's effectua scale. The room ''seems'' too big to this man. What's wrong with the space? It's psychologically too larg

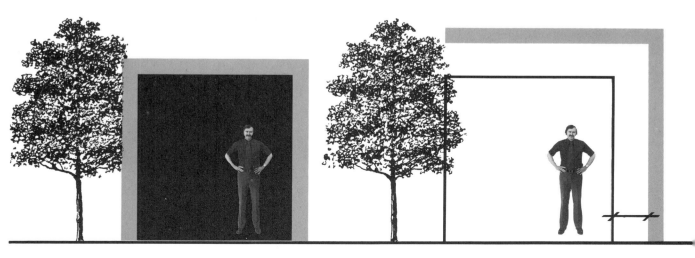

or him. But what if there are a lot of other people in the room with the man (bottom diagram)? Now how will he feel? Probably a lot more comfortable. Psychologically the space is entirely different, although physically it hasn't changed. What has changed is the effectual scale. The space no longer intimidates. The ceiling height is about right to him now that he is part of a group. Effectual scale changes; or more accurately, the effects change depending on the circumstances.

In this example, the space is too large for the person. For 147 people the space may be about the right size. Human scale? It depends on how many humans there are.

It should be pointed out that a lone human being need not necessarily feel overwhelmed by large spaces. Chartres Cathedral (begun in 1194), for example, gives one person a feeling of liberation; to another person the same great interior space might be dehumanizing, if not humbling. Effectual scale? It depends on the person and on the specific time he or she experiences the space.

Since architecture is one person's individual experience, effectual scale is as real to that person as physical scale.

Effectual scale is psychological.

Imagine yourself walking up this tree-lined archway toward a beautiful old Southern mansion. The form you see is familiar. There are the stately columns. The rhythmic dormers. The pleasing proportions. Your expectation of experiencing this old home is great.

But as you get closer and your perception becomes more accurate, you are shocked. What you now see is not an impressive three-story house. It's a one-story bungalow—a house whose *physical scale* is less than one-half the size of the house you thought you were going to experience. You had a certain *associative scale* in the back of your mind—this was a big house you were going to experience. Before you realized that you had been fooled, *effectual scale* took over. You had been deceived by a miniature. This can happen most any place where new ''old southern colonial homes'' have been recently built.

There's no doubt about it. Scale is illusive. Even the yardstick seems to lie at times. Small spaces can look larger than they really are.

In fairness to this beautiful photograph and to an equally fine building, it should be pointed out that this is the real thing—a beautiful three-story Southern mansion.

COMPOSITION

When you appreciate a painting, music, or sculpture, you consciously or subconsciously look or listen to see how skillfully the parts have been put together. You ask yourself: How successful is the composition?

Architects compose with space, form, and light.

With knowledge of technology and developed compositional skills, they compose space and form, which hopefully will result in artistic, functional buildings that cater to changing natural light during the day and electric light at night.

Architects, therefore, must be practical as well as artistic. It's hard enough to compose on a canvas. Or score black dots on staffs to make successful music. Or chip away on pieces of stone to create the perfect sculpture. Or bring the parts of a manuscript together to wrap up an interesting plot. In addition to the artistry, it's even harder to achieve the functional efficiency and the economy required to compose all the parts of a successful building. That is why there are so many banal buildings. The skills of composition and the creativity that go along with them are missing. Excellent buildings require sophisticated compositional skills. The great architects had them. Frank Lloyd Wright, Le Corbusier, Mies van der Rohe, and Louis Kahn developed compositional skills throughout their long careers.

Architectural composition is more than arranging parts like walls, floors, ceiling, roof, windows, and

Left and below: Composition means "to form by putting together." That's quite a job. The architect must have knowledge of engineering in order to be accurate about sizes and affinities of spaces. If not, the building may not perform as it should. He must be technologically right with no room for error. If not, it is a bad shelter, unsafe and uncomfortable, and the users won't like it. And the architect must be artistically capable; if not, his practice will be shortlived because no client wants an eyesore.

Here is the Kimball Art Museum designed by Louis Kahn, whose compositional skills were highly developed. When you walk around this Fort Worth museum, it's like walking around beautiful sculpture. Each step offers a beautiful view. The building is beautiful; and it functions extremely well. Its beauty is reinforced by efficiency.

Above: When you drive into a city for the first time, the fleeting glimpses of individual buildings, the textures and colors of building fabrics, the shapes of the skyline, and the ever-moving composition of space and form make a lasting impression. This series taken from one of Houston's freeways, shows the visual excitement and the shifting geometry of the Pennzoil Building's strong plastic form.

Opposite page: Walk-in sculpture? Right. There is, however, a utilitarian aspect. This structure serves as a fish ladder and as an observation platform. It's located on the river that flows through Grand Rapids, Michigan. You might say that it is living sculpture—a thing of beauty that does something useful. That's the way a building should be.

doors on a sheet of paper. It goes far beyond drawing elevations.

Architectural composition is not the static composition of a painting where the observer stands still. The composition changes whenever the viewer moves. As a person moves through space and around form, the building parts seem to move too. There is one effect when he strolls leisurely through a building. There is another effect when he hurries through a group of buildings on the way to work. And still another effect when he drives the freeway at 55 miles an hour and experiences the changing perspective and shifting geometry of the cityscape.

In composing, architects use any number of design ideas to implement their own intentions. These ideas define the initial character of the building. It's convenient to think of of these ideas in terms of opposing pairs—each idea is applicable at different times and for different purposes. Here are a few examples: *simplicity* versus *complexity* (see page 124), *clarity* versus *ambiguity*, *restraint* versus *exaggeration*.

To emphasize the height of a tall building, the architect might use the idea of *verticality*; to emphasize the floor lines of a tall building, he might use *horizontality*; to provide a surprise and visual pleasure, he might use spatial *contrast* (see page 20) as opposed to *harmony* in adjoining volumes of space. He might use the idea of *rhythm* (see page 50) in window groupings or in columns as opposed to the unpredictability of *randomness.*

Consciously or unconsciously, the architect selects and uses many design ideas—too many to list here. A few more are *unity* versus *disparity, variety* versus *singularity, order* versus (studied) *disorder, symmetry* versus *asymmetry.*

What's best—a symmetrical building or an asymmetrical building? Architects have been debating that question since someone learned to draw a center line. Had an architectural student in the 30s submitted an asymmetrical solution, the professor would have flunked him with a quote from Webster: "Symmetry is the beauty of form arising from balanced proportions." By the 40s symmetry was taboo in the schools. The professors said, "Symmetrical floor plans just don't work." And

The safe way to get architectural unity is to follow the tried and true symmetrical composition recipe:

1. Take a cube.

2. Put it on a platform.

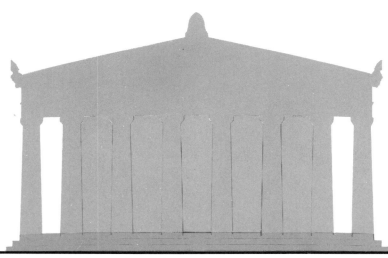

3. Put a lid on it with columns all around.

This recipe was used on the Parthenon.
It's still used today.

generally they don't. Getting a symmetrical balance takes some squeezing—putting half the spaces on the right side of the center line and the other half on the left side. It' a rare case if the total function permits such divisiveness.

During the 60s when monumentality in design made a comeback, a good number of symmetrical compositions appeared on the scene. They were well received, although many architects thought them contrived—form for form's sake. Nevertheless, the public favored the historically familiar symmetrical compositions. Such architects as Edward D. Stone and Minoru Yamasaki, both highly skillful designers, capitalized on this revival. But symmetry has now just about run the popularity course. It'll come back another day.

As the saying goes, the more you work at something, the better you should get. But schools of architecture in America during the 60s and 70s changed curricular emphasis from design to management. The obvious happened. Very few graduates turned out to be skilled designers. Their buildings reflect the lack of developed compositional skills. More experience and education—formal or self-study—are gradually rectifying the situation. There are encouraging signs too that the schools today are going through a design resurgence. If so, there will be more better buildings to appreciate.

6. Physical Environment

Site, light, and building go together to make up the physical environment. They interact.

SITE

The site shapes a building in many ways. Trees and rocks on the site can shape the floor plan. Certain contours can cause a building to look as if it were on stilts, or others can create the need for split-levels. Some buildings on steep sites look like giant steps. The size of the site can also determine the geometry of the building.

People and money are additional building shapers. The people who use the building—the number involved and what they want to do in and around the building—shape the space and set the form. The construction budget also plays a great part in establishing the size and shape of the building, not to mention the quality of the envelope. In fact, architects have told clients, "Your pocketbook is your architect." But the site may prove to be the strongest force to shape a building.

The site, depending upon the location, size, topography, and climate, shapes the space and sets the form. The site, as much as the building on it, creates atmosphere. It can make a bad building look good. A pleasant house nestled among the trees might well look terrible on a treeless prairie.

Site contours sometimes demand unique form and structure. A building designed specifically for a steep slope could not possibly be duplicated on a flat site, and vice versa. A building designed to take advantage of the view of a beautiful waterscape wouldn't do if it were located on the corner of two busy thoroughfares. If the site is rural and large, a one-story structure may be logical. If the site is urban and small, five stories might be best for the same amount of floor area. So remember, site shapes.

Site also establishes the character of the building. If the site is downtown in a large city, that's one thing; if it's in the suburbs on a hill overlooking a scenic lake, that's something else. A building for an urban setting has more neighbors to respect than one located in an isolated area. The urban site requires a completely different exterior treatment and landscaping element. The Guggenheim Museum in New York City was severely criticized as being suitable only for an estate site, not for an urban setting. High-density areas, whether urban or suburban, demand much more of buildings and their grounds because so many people use them.

Urban sites, more often than not, dictate sizes and shapes of buildings because of street patterns, height restrictions, and setbacks. Ocean view, mountain view, and valley view sites usually have buildings that are directional—buildings that look toward the views. Buildings in forests generally open outward to take advantage of the restful, low illumination and adjacent greenery. Most buildings on desert sites open inward, away from the extreme brightness of land and sky and sometimes hostile climate. But some windows are provided for special vistas and panoramas of the vast landscape.

Most people think buildings should have peculiar characteristics related to their region. But what is a region? How large should it be? As big as a country? One-sixth the size of a country like the U.S.? Let's pause to consider this idea. There is a Northwest region (covering the five states listed in *National Geographic's Atlas of the World*).

Opposite page, top: Symmetrical balance is easy for most people to understand. There's historical precedence. The Parthenon is symmetrically composed. Jefferson's Memorial was a symmetrical composition. So does the Lincoln Memorial. So do most state capitols. Symmetry is the tried and true, the most easily perceived. But the Modern Movement in the first decades of the 20th century put a damper on symmetrical composition. The '70s brought on renewed interest in symmetry. The energy crunch stopped that revival, however. Count on it: symmetrical buildings will crop up every so often.

Opposite page, bottom: Asymmetrical compositions are difficult to do. It's hard to achieve balance and good looks at the same time. Desired rhythm and continuity are also difficult to get. The hardest of all is achieving architectural unity. This building does that. To most people it is visually successful. There has been skillful, clear handling of an asymmetrical composition, and sculpture plays an important part in achieving asymmetrical balance.

Above: In addition to composing parts of a single building into a pleasing whole, the architect must create visual unity with the surrounding buildings. Architectural composition ranges from the smallest detail (composing the parts that make up a window) to the largest setting (composing the parts that make up a campus). This example—an interesting composition of masses and space on an expansive walking plane—is the main concourse of The University of Washington in Seattle.

Should that region have a "Northwest architecture" which distinguishes it from a "Southwest architecture"? Before you decide, mull over the facts relating to only one of the five states—Washington. Rainfall varies from 12 feet (3.6 m) a year in the coastal area to a few inches annually on the eastern side of the Cascade Range. Elevation varies from a few inches above sea level in Seattle to 14,410 feet (4,330 m) at the top of Mt. Rainier. Foliage? As much variation. On the eastern side of the mountain there are treeless desert lands, on the western side thick, impenetrable rain forests. Temperature? You name it, Washington has it.

When someone claims that a building should be indigenous to its region, he should define region.

A building designed for one side of the street will not necessarily perform satisfactorily on the other side.

Is a region "across the street"? Microclimatic studies have shown that wintry winds can blow from a different direction on one side of a road than on the other side because of natural barriers (hills, trees) or manufactured barriers (other buildings, fences, landscape elements). Soil surveys show that both topsoil and subsoil conditions can be completely different—one has large boulders and gravel, the other rich earth. Topography too can be startlingly different. One can be flat, while the other drops off sharply.

One site can be part of a thick forest; across the road, the other can have substantially no plant life. Two sites, only 100 feet (30 m) from each other, can demand different kinds of space, form, and construction, even if the functional programs are exactly the same. Site shapes. This point cannot be overemphasized.

Although local conditions may vary dramatically within a region, there is some validity to the concept of regional character, derived originally from the availability of building materials, prevailing climatic and topographical conditions and ways of life. Some recognition of this character may be appropriate in the sensitively handled contemporary building even though technology can overcome the original conditions so that they no longer apply in the same way.

Below: Taliesin West in Arizona, designed by the all-time master of site planning, Frank Lloyd Wright, is a masterpiece. The site works for the user, satisfying emotional needs as well as physical needs. The building doesn't fight the contours of the land as most do. Earth is used as insulation, saving energy. Wright built *with* rather than *against* nature.

Pages 93–95: A feeling of rightness is created when symbiosis exists between site and building.

LIGHT

Architecture depends on light. Almost as much as on space or form. Light paints form, making it visible. Look through a door opening into a dark room. You see opaque blackness—as black as a black door. Flip the light switch. You see space.

Light is the catalyst of space and form.

The presence or absence of light sends signals to the person experiencing the space and form. The signals cause architecture to happen.

A sitting room has a same-size greenhouse adjacent to it. A glass wall separates the two spaces. At night when lights are turned on in the sitting room and no lights are on in the greenhouse, the glass becomes a shiny black opaque wall. With a flick of the switch in the greenhouse, the space is doubled in size. The two rooms become one.

Added light changes the scene.

How light affects form is particularly evident in the contrast between night and day. Less outside light and more inside light change the form. The Seagram Building in New York changes from plastic to skeletal at night. A building in Los Angeles which has plastic form during the day has planar form at night. Many ordinary buildings under daylight become giant lighting fixtures at night. Some that come on visually strong, to the point of bullying their neighborhood during the day, seem to slink away at night. The outside of a windowless building takes on a different visible form during the day than at night; upward spotlights at night define form differently than downward sunlight.

Daylight in New Mexico is quite different from daylight in Maine. For example, buildings in New Mexico under a strong, high sun and glaring sky have high-intensity light which defines form. In Maine where the sun is relatively weak and low, color contrast plays an important role in defining form during daylight hours. During winter's short day, when the sun goes down at midafternoon,

electrical light streaming out the windows helps define outside form. These windows also serve to bring the precious winter sun inside. Light differences, together with differences in temperature, humidity, wind, and precipitation, offer strong reasons for tailoring buildings to specific regions and specific sites within a region.

Architects and collaborating lighting engineers know the nuances between direct lighting (direct from the sun or the lightbulb) and indirect lighting (light bouncing on a surface before illuminating the object). They know how textures can be magnified or diminished. They know how certain forms can be accented by either electric lighting or daylighting. The trick is to get natural light to behave.

Ancient Egyptians, who constructed tombs (some a city block long in solid rock), must have used mirrors to bounce the sunlight deep into the tunnels where the sculptors and painters were working. Oil lamps would have blackened those exquisitely painted bas-reliefs.

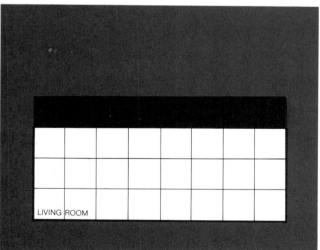

UNLIGHTED TERRACE

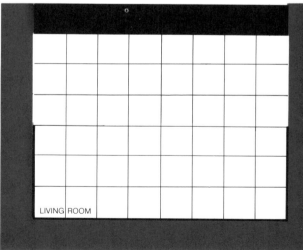

LIGHTED TERRACE

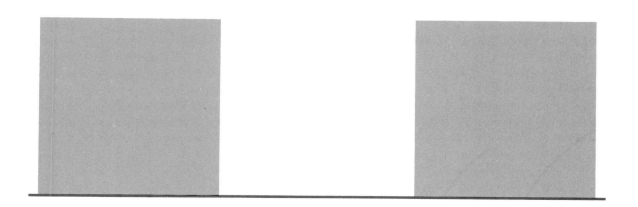

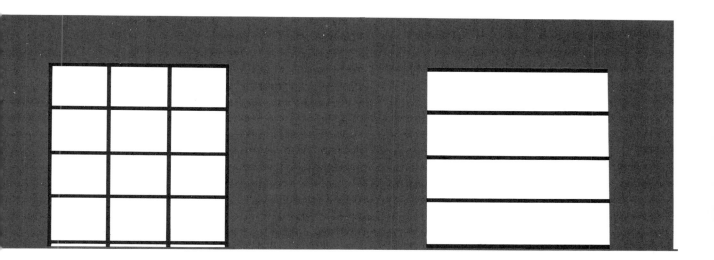

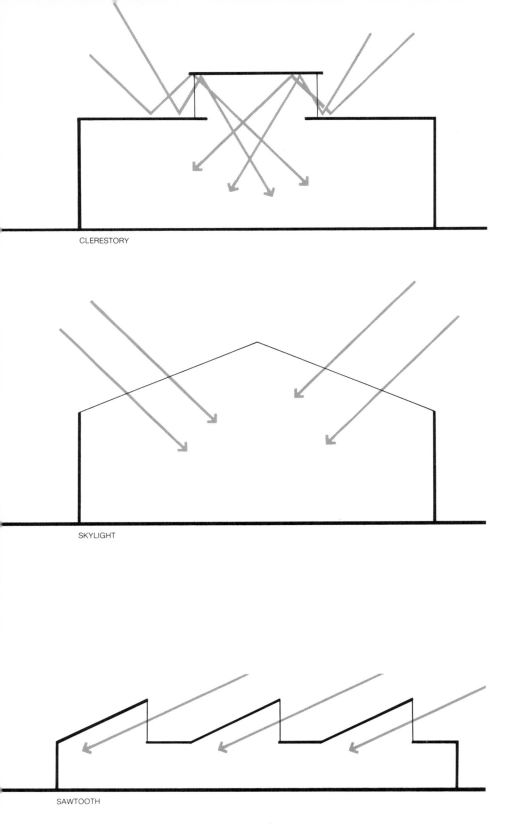

CLERESTORY

SKYLIGHT

SAWTOOTH

Opposite page: Two of the most successful shopping malls—Houston's Galleria (top) and Minneapolis' Crystal Court (bottom)—use the sun and sky, and they do it beautifully. Indubitably, the sun filtering through the skylight on the shoppers below reinforces the architectural experience.

The Egyptians also invented clerestory lighting over 3,000 years ago, give or take a few centuries. The clerestory is the opening created between a wall and a roof through which light is admitted into deep interior spaces. Some Egyptian temples had clerestories 60 feet (18 m) in the air to grab the light from the sun and sky dome. Greek architects used the same technique centuries later. So did the Romans. And the Europeans during the Gothic period.

Architects throughout the ages have designed high windows to let natural light into deep spaces. The higher the better. Cathedrals had the highest. In the middle of the 19th century, skylights were popular ways to make the inside as bright as the outside. The Crystal Palace, designed for the Great Exhibition of 1851 in London, was the largest of such buildings—770,000 sq feet (230,000 sq m).

The sawtooth roof appeared on the scene around the turn of the century as floor areas became necessarily larger, especially in industrial plants. About that time British architects had advanced daylighting to a rather sophisticated level. In this country during the 1940s daylighting research became active. The 50s brought on acres of small, bubblelike plastic skylights. Technology's recent contributions are the giant bubbles (inflatable air structures) of unlimited size made up of translucent, teflon-coated fiberglass. On a bright day, interior lighting within these encapsulated spaces is as much as 600 foot-candles.

Daylighting is both art and science.

Contemporary masters of daylighting as an art were Wright, Le Corbusier, and Louis Kahn. These architects knew how the sun behaved and how buildings should behave under the sun. They created atmospheric beauty with special lighting effects as well as general illumination.

From the standpoint of esthetics electric lighting does not compare with daylighting. Electric lighting systems are fine for providing illumination for work, but for bringing cheer to the worker, sunlight is a lot better.

Natural light is better because it's fluxional. That is its rich quality—variety in change. Changing light changes color, texture, and even shape or form. One little sunbeam can change the entire atmosphere of a room from gloom to cheer. A small window that lets in sun to spotlight a pulpit, a tapestry, or a piece of sculpture is more effective than any commercial lighting fixture. Obviously the sun may not shine at all times; but when it does, it is worth having that hole-in-the-wall to let it in.

The emphasis on daylighting interior spaces changes among architects from decade to decade. During the 50s, followers of Mies did not place much value on daylighting. During the 60s, followers of Kahn did. Practitioners are still doing it during the 70s as artistic expressions of space and form. The art of daylighting is alive and well.

But the science of daylighting has been misplaced. What science the English developed during the last half of the 19th century was lost after the invention of the lightbulb. The 20s and 30s were an awkward transitional period—not enough electric lighting to do the job right and not enough science to make full use of daylight.

It wasn't until the 40s and 50s that the science of daylighting began to evolve again. Natural lighting came back strong. The "new" vogue was the old Egyptian clerestory—bilaterally and trilaterally lighted rooms with light-reflecting louvers, light bubbles, ridge lighting, and skylighting. Daylighting was the name of the game in the 50s.

Above and left: Daylighting is an art and a science. In this Michigan house, architect Gunnar Birkerts brought both into play. Birkerts is one of the first to rekindle interest in the science of daylighting, which was lost during the 60s. Architecture appreciation relates to the vital, ever-changing, natural lighting environment.

Opposite page: During the 50s the CRS team pioneered scientific daylighting. Its work was based on judicious use of glass tested by models in an artificial sky at Texas A&M University (at the time, only Australia had a similar lab). CRS designed schools which required no electricity for lighting during daylight hours; yet because of an advanced technology, the learning spaces, which could be as wide as educators wanted them, were provided with high-level illumination, evenly distributed, glare-free natural lighting. Economical, too. Light from the sun costs less than from the power plant. The school built in the 50s was an energy-efficient building.

These schoolhouses of the 50s were airy and cheerful primarily because they were well lighted by natural means. What a shame when architects and schoolboards advocate windowless schools. What they don't know is that time flows slower with children than adults. The French scientist Lecomte Du Nouy discovered this little known but architecturally important fact. For example, he found out one hour to a 10-year-old child seems three times as long as to a 40-year-old adult. A 10-year-old spends six hours in school. That's equivalent to spending 18 adult hours. The schools shown here are all daylighted by the dynamic light from sky and sun—even in the interior corridor. In fact, lights need not be turned on during the day, saving energy. To put youngsters in windowless schools lighted and ventilated with artificial means is highly questionable as well as energy consuming.

The remarkable fact about this resurgence of daylighting is that the new technology permitted lower ceilings and subsequently less volume which reduced both the cost of construction and the operating cost of the heating system.

Then with the mid-50s came air-conditioning and cheap electricity. Natural lighting went out with the window, and people began to live in windowless boxes under unchanging, dull, electric-lighted ceilings. The science of daylight was mothballed. The art of daylighting took a beating, although a few architects like Kahn bucked the trend toward a completely artificial environment.

Kahn was right. The current energy shortage proves natural lighting must be given prime consideration in the design of buildings. And more importantly, people have a deep-seated need for the amenities of natural lighting.

Lighting interior spaces by natural means produces unusual and pleasing effects. This is caused first by the light itself which brings life into the spaces by the movement of sun and clouds and second by the design of the skylight which creates interesting, fresh, new forms.

7. Psychological Environment

During the last two decades buildings have become increasingly complex. Jesse H. Jones Hall for the Performing Arts in Houston, Texas (below), is disarmingly simple. Behind those straightforward facades, inside the partitions themselves, above the ceiling and surrounding the stage, there's enough machinery and electronic equipment for a battleship. Desert Samaritan Hospital in Mesa-Tempe, Arizona (opposite page), fools the eye. It too is intricate. As medical science has advanced, hospitals have become so complex they've begun to take on the characteristics of a super lab with wall-to-wall scientific equipment.

If you know a little about the problems a building is solving, you'll appreciate that building just a little more. Jones Hall can be tuned like a violin. Samaritan Hospital tries to help the patient get well faster and home quicker. Neither is a simplistic solution.

Buildings today are too complex for one person to design. It takes a team of specialists. Late in his life, Le Corbusier openly gave credit to his team. In fact, about the time of his death, he was investigating the computer as a means of analyzing directions in design approach.

The thought and creativity that go into a building these days comes gestaltlike from many specialists: the conceptual designer, the building type consultant, the programmer, the interior designer, the landscape architect, the civil engineer, the estimator, the building systems specialist, the acoustical engineer, the mechanical engineer, the electrical engineer, the construction manager, the specifications writer, the design developer, the construction administrator. And the list goes on.

The newest members of the architectural team to appear on the design scene are the behavioral scientists—generally psychologists and sociologists. Since the arrival of these specialists in the mid-60s, there's been a great deal of excitement in the design profession. Architects, who love vagueness, abstractness, and beautiful ambiguous phrases, were to hear the behavioral people produce such verbal gems as "the rich behavior setting," "coercive forces," "behavior input," "the perceived environment," "perceived density," "environmental quality," "holistic view," and "the effective environment of human behavior."

But architects have had second thoughts. Were behaviorists intruding on their territory? Would they take over and run the show? Or would they give a better balance to the design teams which were prone to overemphasize the physical?

Should the architect be afraid of people who discovered that buildings are so important that the way a door swings can affect people's happiness by making them feel isolated or socially integrated? In a museum a door can compete with the paintings, the sculpture, even other people. Bad buildings can contribute to suicides; good buildings can help prevent them. Round rooms encourage social intercourse. Old people in nursing homes die sooner in rooms at the end of halls.

Buildings affect the behavior of people.

Buildings are important. However, sociologists and psychologists seem to agree that in dealing with user stress and satisfaction, buildings rank no higher than fourth place after user motivation, manage-

Every user in a newly occupied building can adapt to his environment through learning. In the CRS office building, people park on the roof and take the elevator *down* to the office level. At first this caused confusion; it's normal to go *up*. But learning soon overcame experience, and after a few mistakes, people learned to go *up* to their parked cars.

Materials speak. They send visual messages: "I'm cold"; "I'm warm and friendly." This is Pima College in Tucson, Arizona, which has two main materials—concrete and steel panels. The architects anticipated that students would consider the concrete as warm since it recalls the color and texture of the surrounding desert. They also thought the students might think the steel panels on the peripheral corridors were cold. The architects were surprised to find the students considered steel warm and concrete cold.

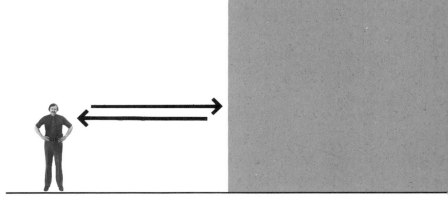

A building and a person interact. You act on it, and it acts on you.

ment, and policies. Still, this does not detract from the premise that buildings are important. People do respond positively or negatively to space and form; so buildings should be designed by architects who know how users respond. Even more important, architects should know how to achieve user satisfaction related to the physical environment, particularly how the user will react to sensory stimuli—light, sound, touch, smell.

Heinz von Foerster, both a physical and behavioral scientist who is replacing Marshall McLuhan as the current hero of young architects, said this to a group of architects in Atlanta in 1975:

"When we perceive our environment, it is we who invent it."

Very basic. Architects don't "invent" the physical environment as much as they would like to think. You do—the user. Von Foerster reinforced this with, "You do not perceive what you do not perceive." In other words, you don't know what you are missing.

So if you don't like a building, maybe you should think about *why* you don't like it. Always remember that a person and a building interact. It takes two. You and the building. If you are dead, emotionally or intellectually, the building will "play dead." If you desire to perceive, learn how to interact. Let yourself go.

One way is to think of a building in the anthropomorphic sense. Does it love you? Hate you? Is it fat or thin? Does it have a brutalism that intimidates you? Or is it meek? Is it a show-off, trying to flex its muscles? Is it nervous, enough to make you nervous? Or does it have a calming effect? Is it friendly? Is it vulgarly ostentatious? Does it have dignity? Is it sociable? Antisocial?

The user interacts with and affects a building.

Winston Churchill made the famous statement, "We shape our buildings and thereafter our buildings shape us." He was right; but there's more to it. People do not merely perceive and *react* to their environment; they also *interact* with it.

New buildings don't always suit the people who use them; the users often modify the interior to suit themselves. In effect they reshape their environment.

A man in a prison cell will establish his individuality by covering the bare walls.

A person in an apartment will modify the environment with paint or pictures.

A manager will transform a suite of offices. In fact, the concept of convertibility in office buildings (open planning) is intended to allow people and space to adapt to each other to achieve a variety of goals.

However, people don't interact the same way. So don't expect your neighbor to like your house just because you do. Although the behavioral scientist on the design team can help identify the differences in people's value systems, it's no easy task. Users, managers, owners, and even spectators or occasional visitors, each interact with a building in different ways depending on his or her previous experience, knowledge, and stages of personal development.

What do people like? For one thing, many people do not like buildings that architects like. Most people make evaluations based on previous experience, which means they place a lot of value on tried-and-true forms. However, given time to learn and develop, people can change their first evaluation. So don't be afraid of a new, strange form. Most people hated the Eiffel Tower when it was first constructed. So too with the United Nations Building. And Brahms' Second Symphony.

Immediate and general public acceptance is hardly the criteria for good art, good music, and good buildings precisely because it implies the veneration of old and established forms. And forms can get old and tired very quickly. To maintain the status quo stifles the development of any art or science. So it is a rather neat feat for a creative architect to develop new and valid architectural forms that people will like immediately and will continue to like.

Like great art, great buildings raise appreciation levels.

The behavioral scientist's most valuable contribution is probably helping architects determine those values, goals, and concepts which in-

fluence form. The form-givers—those elements that give physical, solid shape to a building—must be identified even before the architectural sketches are started. Here's where behavioral people on the design team can be a big asset. And they are also needed during attempts to measure a building's performance.

It's a good bet architects and behavioral scientists will collaborate more in the future. Architects need to find out more about you. You, as the user, are the one who counts. Your interaction with architecture is what's important.

When you judge a building, what is the issue?

In judging a building, try to establish how well it responds to its intended purpose. To be a good or even a great building it must have some measure of universality. For example, the immediate occupants may not want privacy, but the next generation may want it. A building, therefore, should have certain qualities of convertibility.

Large buildings with many users, such as concert halls, museums, hospitals, and particularly schools, affect the identity of the individual. It is said that an individual loses his identity in a large group. The question arises: With how many people can an individual identify and still preserve his self-image? The answer must come from sociology or organizational psychology. It will affect, first, the size of the groups and, second, the organization of spaces in a building. Suppose the answer is: an individual can identify with 500 people in this particular situation. The behavioral solution to the problem created by 2,000 people is then to decentralize the mass into four groups of 500 people each. The building is then planned to house the four separate groups in four distinct building units. So when you see a decentralized school, hospital, or the like, know that there are reasons—right or wrong—behind this physical separation. You may want to know what the reasons are. Knowing may increase (or decrease) your appreciation of the building.

Think about a new building you visited for the first time. Did you feel lost? Some visitors to certain build-

Above: Consecration of a building has deep historical roots. It's a way to show how important the new building is. To show how it can help people perform the function to which it is dedicated. This photograph was taken during the consecration of a hospital in Zuni, New Mexico, which was built expressly to improve health care for the Indian community. Such an event carries the overtone of ownership by a mass of people. Ownership encourages architecture to happen.

Pages 109–110: If a building doesn't quite suit the user, the person or persons sometimes modify it the way they want it. In effect they reshape the environment so it "belongs" to them. Since buildings are for and of people, they must be adaptable to changing human needs. Architects are prone to make buildings too finished so there is nothing left for the users to do. The user must "build his own nest," make his own home base if the building is an office, school, or apartment complex. There must be a sense of ownership. It would be interesting to know why the owner of this barn (opposite page) painted it as he did. You can bet there was a good reason, related to individualizing a building that looked like everyone else's. Note how the children (page 110) redecorated their assembly hall with surplus parachutes. Think how much more they can appreciate it. It's theirs now.

ings are completely disoriented after taking a few steps, yet these buildings were supposedly designed to receive and take care of visitors. If it is important to have visitors, the building or group of buildings must provide clear, easy-to-understand circulation lanes. Another way of minimizing that lost feeling is for the building to have reference points such as a court, a fountain, a sculpture—some predominant item. Good orientation from the users' point of view is a desired quality in any building.

Any effort towards analyzing a building pays off. You also learn more about yourself.

OWNERSHIP
Think a bit about the psychology of ownership.

Why does a person appreciate his own house? The predominant reason is that it is "his own house." He may not own the house outright; he may be renting it. Nevertheless, it's "his own house" because, for one reason or another, it belongs to him. A person who is involved in the design process of a new building or who has adapted an existing building to fit his physical, emotional, and intellectual needs will generally have a strong attachment to that building—a feeling of ownership.

Human values concerning buildings often relate to ownership.

This attachment is one way in which architecture happens. How does a person "own" the building? It might well be that he "owns" a room in the building. It's his territory. His piece of real estate. His nest. He feels comfortable in it.

A man converts his garage into a den—a retreat to get away from his son's loud rock-and-roll tapes and his wife's continuous TV. The den is primarily a listening area for his unusual collection of organ music. The man, an engineer, designed the space himself. Furnished it himself. Successful in every way—effective sound isolation, sound reverberation just right, and esthetically correct to fit his personal taste. To this man, it is a great place to be—it's "his own place." To him it is architecture.

Another person enters the room for the first time. She is appalled by the visual disorder, the garish colors, the generally overall "poor taste." To her it's a bad scene. Not architecture for her.

Who's right? The man or the visitor? To the man there is architecture. To the visitor there isn't. Yet both are right because architecture (back to the definition) is a *personal*, enjoyable, necessary experience. Fortunately, in this case it is the man's den, and isn't he the only one who really counts? Architecture exists for him. He's proud of his den.

He built it with his own hands. It turned out just like he wanted it to.

Ask yourself these questions: Just because the man likes his room, does that make it successful? Yes, for him. Does it possess architecture? Yes, to him. Doesn't architecture go beyond the feelings of personal ownership? Yes, but by definition if this man thinks there is architecture, there is architecture. You may argue that there has to be an element of objective judgment as well as personal emotional reaction in calling something architecture. You're right, but his judgment is made on low-level evaluative criteria. On the other hand, the visitor probably has had many opportuni-

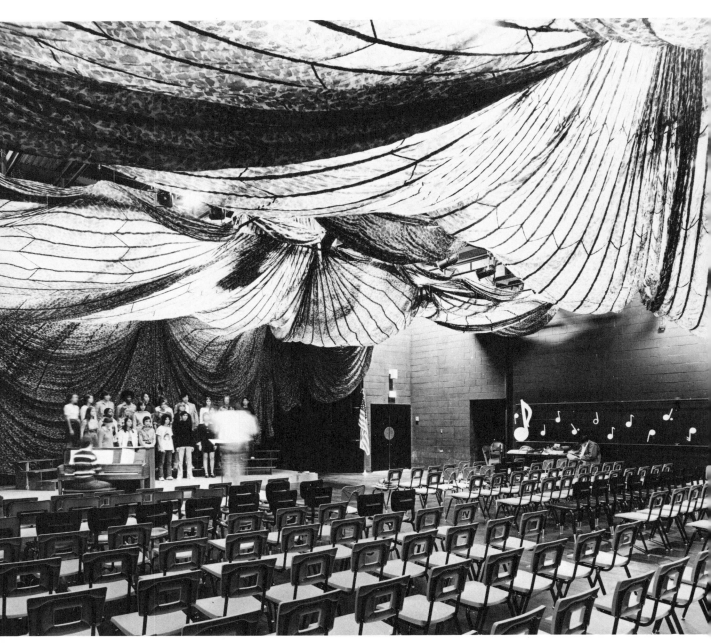

ties in experiencing great buildings and has developed high-level evaluative criteria. This room does not possess architecture to her.

Reflect on the statement in Chapter 5 that imitation of styles is bad. Yet you know that some people are very happy with them. And you know why: these people lack knowledge of historical style—the whats, whys, and hows. It's the same kind of ignorant bliss that this man has. He's happy about his retreat because he has nothing to compare it with. No high-level evaluative criteria.

You can argue too that if the man has any self-knowledge or sophistication, he would know that the rea-

son he likes his den is because it's the only place that he controls. That might be reason enough for architecture to exist in his mind. He may be deluded into thinking the space has a special quality tailored just for him. Deluded or not, if he loves the space, that's all that matters—architecture exists.

It's much easier for people to condone mediocrity of their own doing than to tolerate the poor quality of others. Ownership makes architecture happen when nothing else will.

The man's den might well be a symbol to him. Not many men in his neighborhood have dens. This puts him a notch above the others.

Below: A school, regardless of its pleasing proportions, stimulating colors, and exciting technology, has no architecture if it's empty. The children and teachers activate architecture because architecture concerns the chemistry between building and user. If the user likes it, then there is architecture. If he likes it, he has probably taken it over as his own, adapting space and form to his benefit and pleasure. If the user feels that he owns the place, that it's his territorial domain, then architecture is assured.

SYMBOLISM

Certain building forms are symbolic. A church steeple is a symbol. There was a time when a Christian church was not a church if it didn't have a steeple. Other religious symbols are minarets (Islamic), "onion domes" (Russian), and the crossless "Baptists boxes" which mushroomed in the U.S. Bible belt in the 20s. At the turn of the century, banks had to look like Greek temples, solid and strong. No one would dare rob a temple. Today apartment houses try to look like French chateaus, with the ghost of architect Francois Mansart hovering over them. Are they symbols of gracious living, these caricatures of French chateaus? Or symbolic nostalgia?

Periodically there is a nostalgia movement which runs counter to progress in creativity; however, the recreated style is never as good as the original. For example, the Greek Revival never equaled the original

nor did the Collegiate Gothic match the great cathedrals.

Europeans look at U.S. skyscrapers as symbols—"temples of commerce." During the 20s every small city had to have a skyscraper That was a symbol of progress. No respectable city would be caught without one. In the 60s the upper-middle-class family had as its symbol of success a facsimile of an Old English country house (in the city a well as in the suburbs) with a Cadillac parked in front. It's about the same today, except the Cadillac ha been replaced by a van. It's human nature to be phony at times, but:

Phoniness erodes logical form.

It always has; always will. According to some deep-thinking architects, specifically Robert Venturi and Denise Scott Brown, phoniness is real Not bad, they say.

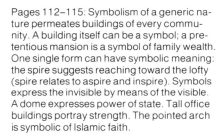

Pages 112–115: Symbolism of a generic nature permeates buildings of every community. A building itself can be a symbol; a pretentious mansion is a symbol of family wealth. One single form can have symbolic meaning: the spire suggests reaching toward the lofty (spire relates to aspire and inspire). Symbols express the invisible by means of the visible. A dome expresses power of state. Tall office buildings portray strength. The pointed arch is symbolic of Islamic faith.

Overembellished, Versailles-fla-
red flowerpots, fake mansard
ofs, plaster arches that don't hold
anything, and stairs that lead no-
here communicate social status,
cording to these scholarly archi-
cts. They maintain that these are
mbols that give vitality to the oth-
wise sterile scene—overplanned
mmunities and their monotonous
sual order. They argue that the log-
al can be banal. They have a point.
rhaps there is something to the
tion that *schlock* warms the soul
d feeds the ego. In any case
hlock prevails—everywhere. In
s Vegas it's the Strip. In Houston,
the get-culture-quick row hous-
g with the paste-on facades. What
t in your own town?

What if people want and like this
rt of thing? If that is what it takes to
ve architecture, so be it. Archi-
cture is more important than archi-
cts who have certain notions
out what people should like. How-
er, living in a culture of phoniness
s no long-range benefits. It's fun
ile it lasts, but it doesn't last long.
en more important:

**oniness is a revelation of
e thinness of the culture.**

An advanced culture needs serious
buildings as much as it needs serious music, serious visual arts, and
serious performing arts. By accept-
ing phoniness, architects abdicate
their professional responsibilities
and are permissive, prostituting their
beliefs and goals.

Some architects propose that
buildings be "concrete expressions
of their time." Nice sounding rhet-
oric, but what if "their time" is a period of social upheaval, threats of
war and disillusionment? Should
buildings look "their time"—nervous? This is another one of those
other-side-of-the-coin philosophies
which hopefully will wear itself out.
Who wants to live in a "nervous"
building, even if it is symbolic of the
times? A person who is insecure and
nervous needs to go home to a
quiet, restful, secure atmosphere.
Architects can create such an atmosphere.

Thank goodness for those townhouses, condominiums, apartments, and single-family houses that
have innovative vitality, honest styling, dignity, warmth, and livability
which convey personal identity.
Hopefully, the current display of
phoniness will soon run ints course.
But be ready for something else.
There will always be illogical form.

Before you decide you do or don't like this building (the Mummers Theater in Oklahoma City), read what a jury of architects said after giving it an award in 1972: "The whole complex works beautifully. More than that, it is an extraordinary, fresh and provocative work of architecture—rational, but wonderfully witty; mechanistic but joyfully humane." This doesn't mean you have to like it, but it does show that architect John Johansen has peers who do. *Architectural Forum* of March 1971 stated, "If the theater in America as an art form is to survive the flicks and TV, it can do so only if it becomes a vital and vibrant expression of the American scene—the high-style as well as the low-style scene." The building and the people connected with it had tough going; nevertheless, the theater has had its influence.

It's a raw, crude building, one in which theater groups can do just about anything. It's nervous, but exciting. In some ways it's a phony and a show-off. But isn't theater that way? Ask yourself: Shouldn't a building that houses drama be symbolic of what's happening inside? Shouldn't it inspire actors and stage designers? Buildings like this one keep us out of a mental rut. When a controversial, new building appears on the scene, keep an open mind. Study it thoroughly before making a judgment. It may be proven later to be innovative, having a sustaining quality. Many famous paintings and musical compositions were rejected when they were first introduced to the public. Try to distinguish between irresponsible imagination and significant creativity.

COLOR

Think a bit about the psychology of color.

Red walls seem to move forward; blue walls recede. Most architects were told about this phenomenon when they were students. If it doesn't work for you, don't worry. It's never been proven. The reason? People are different. Confronted with a red wall one person, because of his history of experiencing color and his color sensitivity, reacts differently from another person with different experiences and sensitivity.

Color cannot be isolated from its source of perception. Josef Albers, American artist and educator, is reported to have sent 50 students into the same street to find examples of "Coca-Cola red" and received 50 different answers. This sort of thing does not bother researchers. They keep on researching.

Researchers get excited about the possibility of the color of a room making people warmer without changing the thermostat. They may be able to prove this for many people. If someone suggested that a certain color was "fiery red," chances are it would seem hot to you. If you are told a color is "cheery yellow," it would probably seem cheery. If someone labels a color "cool green," you'll probably believe it.

It's not so much a case of seeing is believing as it is believing is seeing.

A suggestive label leads to believing. But this doesn't necessarily mean everyone will see it that way. What's important is how *you* see color. The more you know about yourself and your color biases, the better understanding you'll have of yourself and a building. Keep remembering that architecture appreciation concerns the chemistry between a building and you.

There's a building in Los Angeles that is shiny blue. Very controversial. When the architect was asked, "Why blue"? he was said to have replied, "Would it look better red?" By most evaluative criteria concerning function, form, economy and time (not color), this building ranks high among architects. Would having it red, yellow, or pink make a difference to you? It's a guess, but most of those people who hate the building would probably like it if it were white. So color does count. But that's up to you. It's your choice.

You cannot isolate color from its source of perception—from you.

Prepare yourself for future color shock. Architects are getting bored with "gray on gray" and "white on white." In Allentown, Pennsylvania, there's a medical center that is red and blue on the outside, blue and gold on the inside. What do those colors mean to you? "Slow death" or "get well"? Architects love to intellectualize color with rationales as beautiful as their colors. It's worth a listen. Your color bias, if not comprehension, may change. You may not be a color expert, but you are the expert on you. This does not mean you should stop learning about color. The more you know, the more fun you'll have appreciating buildings. Color evokes emotional and physical response. Physical? Sure, paint your dark green room white and the illumination level will be raised considerably.

Architects have found that color behaves in most interesting ways. Clients are almost always fooled when they select a certain color from a small color chip to be applied to a large area. A woman who chooses the color of her living room from a red thread she pulled out of her lamp shade will suffer color shock. A color of a certain hue and lightness appears quite different in interior spaces than in exterior spaces. A color looks different in direct light and indirect light. It's different in early morning than at high noon. Size matters. A small area will not look the same as a large area of the same color.

A cotton-judging establishment served a district consisting of several plantations. One year the crops produced a much lower grade of cotton, the grading being determined by its whiteness. "Why?" The farmers asked. Soil, seed, and rainfall had not changed materially from the year before. Someone finally solved the mystery. The large north windows of the cotton laboratory, faced a high wood fence. During the year the fence had been painted red. Red reflected into the laboratory making the cotton appear less white than normal and therefore of poorer quality due to its reddish tint.

Another case of physical effect: A convention center in a southwest city has a large dining hall carpeted with a bright orange rug. Walls and ceiling are white. But the walls are not the same white they were before the carpet was installed. The ceiling, particularly, was affected. When the lights were turned on, sending beams downward, the rug turned back the light to the ceiling, giving it a pronounced orange hue.

A bucket of paint goes a long way in changing the physical environment. When school architects in the 1950s switched from "schoolhouse brown" to bright, lively colors, children began to take more interest in their surroundings and, according to many teachers, more interest in their studies. After a group of children moved from the dull, drab environment of their old, obsolete schoolhouse to a skillfully conceived and developed new building, one child remarked, "I wish I lived here." She didn't realize it, but she spent more daylight hours in her new school than in her home. Another child, a third grader, said in reference to his classroom, "It's like springtime." It was midwinter. Colors made the difference.

The emotional aspect and the physical aspect are both strong considerations in how you respond to color. The more you know about both aspects, the more you can appreciate color in the architecture experience.

8. Societal Needs

Buildings, in one way or another, reveal the culture of a people. This is true of primitive people, true of advanced societies. Compare the buildings of the aborigines on an isolated island of New Guinea with those of people on the island of Britain. If you study housing in Central America, in Middle Africa, in the Scandinavian countries, in Japan, and in this country, you can see societal differences. These differences relate to needs and aspirations. A visitor to the U.S., unfamiliar with our educational system, is amazed at the abundance of community colleges—strictly an American invention. This tells a good deal about values placed by the U.S. on public education.

In Europe the change in size of concert halls from the small, intimate ones for royal courts to those with large capacities of 2,000 or 3,000 seats indicates the spread of appreciation of the performing arts from the royal elite to mass audience groups. These larger concert halls represent the cultural values in a democratic society, if not, certainly the rise in affluence of the middle class.

When people move from farms to cities, buildings reflect this change. The switch from the individual home to the apartment house, townhouse, or condominium represents more than land shortages, transportation difficulties, and inflation. Desire for cluster living also causes change in building types and shapes. The more recent movement from the cities to the rural areas shows that this nation, which was a nation of immigrants, seems now to be one of continuing internal migration. Its people are always on the move, seeking better jobs and amenities. This explains particularly those paste-on-front townhouses. The nomads are trying to find instant roots as well as instant roofs.

Society affects buildings and vice versa.

A filling station on every corner tells in no uncertain terms what value

Pages 119–120: From its beginning this country put education high on its hierarchy of values. America invented the community college to help solve the problem of education beyond high school; the movement took hold in the 60s. Buildings are telling evidence of how a society deals with its problems.

society places on the automobile as the chief means of transportation. It tells other things: that a car is more than transportation—it's a symbol. Everybody who is anybody should have one; people are mobile and affluent. The trend to protect the car from the elements and thieves by closing in carports tells us of people's increasing dependence on it. Buildings tattle.

The influx of apartment groups, condominiums, complete with swimming pools, lighted tennis courts, singles clubs, and dining facilities indicate drastic changes in lifestyles. New churches that are springing up everywhere provide an accurate scoreboard as to what is happening in religion. Look at the increasing number of new tennis clubs, and you'll know something about what is happening in recrea-

ion. Look at all those hospitals built
in the 60s and early 70s. You will see
evidence of the value government
placed on health care. Visit some of
the new retirement villages; you will
have a more accurate story of what
is happening than any demographic
report. Visit new factories; you'll see
"people places," reflecting a huma-
nistic approach to the industrialized
process. Tour some new correction-
al facilities (only a very short visit,
please), and you'll easily detect the
current change in philosophy of
rehabilitating prisoners. Buildings
are good storytellers. They reveal
needs and society's responsive-
ness.

The building boom of the 50s and
60s attempted to fulfill societal
needs. The physical need for putting
more roofs over more bodies was
paramount. But attitudinal change
was another impelling force, perhaps as strong.

It was the post-war dream to
take care of everybody.

This covered all aspects of society.
Manifestation of this dream came
close to reality in education, although health care was a close second. Look at schools. They can tell
you what's going on in education.
One of the most vital periods of
American education blossomed in
the 50s, although it was started
much earlier. John Dewey stood out
among many as the philosophical
leader of educational reforms. He
wanted action-oriented schools.
The old Scottish architects of those
great fortress-like castles had a saying, "The container should equal the
contained." Dewey would have said
this was particularly true of a school.

everyone is aware of the time a typical com-
muter spends going from home to work and
back on freeways and crowded backroads.
The journey has to be made less monotonous, more pleasant. And energy must be
conserved. Despite the noble attempt of a
few cities like San Francisco to help solve the
transportation problem through rapid transit,
automobiles continue to ruin cities. When
freeways and streets are clogged, the cities
possess no architecture. City dwellers have
as much right to architecture as those dwellers of the countryside. They can have the excitement of moving trains that have purpose
and order and can help provide architecture
on a large physical scale. But just getting rid
of cars won't solve the problem. The trains
and stations must love people.

The school boom followed the baby boom. Douglas Haskell of *Architectural Forum* aptly described the early 50s by describing the situation as ''The thundering herd of the patter of little feet.'' U.S. architects responded. The problem of putting a roof over children's heads was hard enough, but educators wisely wanted more. They wanted the school to perform as an efficient teaching machine. Even more, they wanted it to be a place of inspiration conducive to learning. What they really wanted was architecture for children.

The switch from the intense construction of schools to hospitals came in the 60s. Almost every community got one—some with architectural quality. Before that, patients and their families and friends endured buildings that were foreboding, antiseptically cold, and jail-like. Someone finally discovered the patient. Then came more pleasant environments along with more efficient spaces.

9. Economy

A building is a solution to a certain group of problems concerning programmatic and functional needs. The intent is for the building to respond to those needs—to help the users do whatever they need to do, be it worshipping or manufacturing a TV set. In any case there is always the obvious consideration—efficiency of function. The building has to function, do the job it's supposed to do, and do it well. There is a second consideration not so obvious to most people—economy.

Economy is maximum effect with minimum means.

SIMPLICITY
Economy implies simplicity. Simplicity was a desired quality long before The Bauhaus (a design school established in Germany in 1919 which emphasized simplicity as part of its philosophy of design). In 1897 Adolf Loos said, "The lower a nation's cultural level, the more lavish its ornaments." Louis Sullivan, five years before, had talked about buildings "beautiful in their nakedness." In 1850, before Louis Sullivan, Horatio Greenough said, "The redundant must be pared down, the superfluous dropped, the necessary itself reduced to its simplest expression, and then we find . . . that beauty was waiting." These people advocated visual economy.

The other side of this coin is the notion that complexity is enrichment. That simplicity is dull. That "less is a bore," not "less is more." That simple buildings lack excitement and vitality. That buildings should have ambiguity. That without ambiguity, there can be no mystery, no visual excitement. That straightforward, no-nonsense, clear solutions to a design problem leave nothing for intellectual stimulation.

The case for complexity and related ambiguity has been eloquently made by Robert Venturi in his book *Complexity and Contradiction in Architecture* published in 1966. Of course, some buildings should have richness. Perhaps complexity. Even a degree of ambiguity. The Seagram Building, in New York City, designed by Mies van der Rohe with Philip Johnson, has an ambiguous, if not an ambivalent, quality at dusk when interior lighting begins to define the grid of the facade. It's a moving experience watching the great giant change its total-form within a matter of a few minutes—from plastic form to skeletal form. It should be made clear, however, that its total-form under normal light—day and night— is not indecisive. It approaches pure plastic form in daylight and pure skeletal form at night. Most buildings' total-form is wishy-washy in this respect. They don't know what they want to be—a quality of ambiguity certainly not desirable. The viewer yearns for clear expression. First-rate buildings speak in no uncertain terms with clarity and simplicity. Mediocre buildings stutter.

The underlying quality of most great buildings has been elegant simplicity.

Simplicity applies to painting, sculpture, literature, and music as well. Leonard Bernstein, referring to Beethoven's Fifth Symphony, said, "Every time I look at this orchestral score, I am amazed all over again at its simplicity, strength, and rightness. And how economical the music is." If architecture is visual music, as some professors have described it, then buildings should have this same quality of economy. Even more so.

Here is a modern architectural masterpiece— the Seagram Building in New York, designed by Mies van der Rohe in association with Philip Johnson. Built in 1958, it has sustaining quality that should last for years to come, primarily because of its stately simplicity of mass and the exquisitely detailed connections.

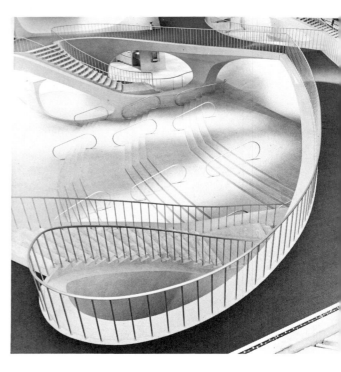

During the design process most architects start with complexity and work toward simplicity. They never quite get there in the never-ending process. There are no perfect solutions. The best solutions are simple, even obvious answers to difficult functional and esthetic problems. The greatest compliment you can give an architect is to say, "Your building is a simple, natural solution." If this "simple, natural solution" is artistically designed (as in these photographs), the object (be it a house, church, or chair) will likely possess those qualities that cause architecture to happen with lasting effect.

131

Simple forms foster dignity. Simple forms give
sustaining quality.

Simple forms create visual excitement.
Simple forms communicate.

What kind of simplicity are we talking about? The clarity of visual expression? If so, are we talking about total-form or details? About restraint from ornamentation? Mies' German Pavilion (top) had admirable elegant simplicity. It must have had a terrific impact on visitors who attended the International Exposition in Barcelona, Spain, in 1929 and saw this unusual building. Other buildings there had familiar, comfortable forms adorned with popular geegaws. Mies believed in the inherent richness of material, not in applied ornamentation.

In discussing simplicity are we talking about economic directness that uses materials in a straighforward way (right) without contrived mannerisms? Are we talking about a building being free of pretense— being what it is, nothing more? Are we talking about a mystic something that gives simplicity even to complexity—as fresh snow covers all the hard edges, distracting details, and ugliness? It's probably all of these. Beethoven's Fifth Symphony is rich in details; yet there's a great overriding simplicity.

The Parthenon (447–438 B.C.) in Athens is credited with perfect proportions. Rightly so, in the case of stone construction, but it's not a perfect building. There are none. Buildings are like people; this one happens to be very beautiful, but with a few blemishes, like carvings that look like wood construction. You take the bad with the good. This one has a lot of good.

COST

Economy relates to cost. There has always been and always will be concern for monetary economy. Marcus Vitruvius Pollio, a Roman architect, stated (about 40 B.C.) that principles of design related to ''eurythmy, symmetry, propriety and economy.''

Architects are still learning from those Greeks—Ictinus and Callicrates, the leading architects of the Acropolis in Periclean Athens. Throughout the ages, architects have pilgrimaged up the steep slope of the Acropolis—particularly to study its dominating Parthenon. Le Corbusier spent months studying the nuances of its refinement—the exquisitely detailed and machinelike finishes of the prefabricated columns, the perspective-correcting curvature of the cornice, and the esthetic system in stone.

The Parthenon enjoys the reputation of being the most perfect building ever built. It comes close. But is it perfect? If it were perfect, would there be the vestiges (dentils) of its wood predecessors? Shouldn't a stone building look like stone, and not have wood joinery? But this carryover is understandable. Like animals and birds, buildings have their evolution. If there can be toes on bird wings, why shouldn't there be dentils on the Parthenon? Since all buildings are imperfect, you need to carry with you some tolerance when experiencing space and form.

A more serious criticism of the Parthenon might well be: It cost too much. That's not as silly as you

Below: The largest of the Great Pyramids at Gizeh was named after the ruler Cheops, or Khufu (2680 B.C.), whose reign is associated with the mystery of the Sphinx.

Opposite page: Considered one of the most beautiful buildings in the world, the Taj Mahal at Agra, India, was erected by Sháh Jehán in 1630. It is as beautiful by night as by day.

might think. The architects got into serious trouble. Some historians have said that the Parthenon helped cause the downfall of the Athenian empire. If so, what a cost that was.

Go back further—to ancient Egypt and the great pyramids. According to the records, the big one, Cheops, required 20 years and 400,000 men (apparently encouraged by overseers with whips in hand) to build it. Wonder what the "person in the street" thought of that project. Herodotus said, "Cheops brought the people to utter misery." If so, that's a high price to pay.

The beautiful Taj Mahal contributed to the decline of the Moguls. Its architect got into hot water too because that super jewel box cost too much—money that could have been

spent on better things for the welfare of the country.

When you think of the real cost (not just the monetary cost) of the Parthenon, the pyramids, the Taj Mahal, and even some of the Gothic cathedrals (the sacrifices peasants made to produce them), don't they seem a little less beautiful?

Perhaps you are too detached. If so, come closer to home. Knowing that those antebellum Southern mansions were built, in many cases, by slaves, some of whom sacrificed their lives to produce those lovely homes, do you still think they are lovely? You hear people say, "Why can't they build buildings now like they used to?" "No slaves, that is why." Not a bad answer. And that's why buildings today cost so much.

Why can't a building be like an Eames chair?
Fine lines. Beautiful proportions. Simple,
but not simplistic. Of quality materials, but not
expensive. Takes advantage of industrialization, yet has design excellence. This
molded and bent birch plywood low side
chair designed by Charles Eames and built by
Herman Miller Inc. in 1946 is loved by old architects, especially anyone who owned one.
In the early 50s it was one of the few pieces of
furniture of design excellence they could afford.

No slaves. And that's why people appreciate labor-saving building methods. That's why we like to get the most for the money, why we see beauty in efficiency and economy.

Try this question: What do you appreciate the most? A Volkswagen or a Rolls Royce? That's a tough one.

Yet we have Volkswagen buildings and Rolls Royce buildings and everything in between. Is it right to measure them with the same esthetic yardstick? For efficiency and economy, a Volkswagen is hard to beat. For luxury and engineering sophistication, they don't come much better than a Rolls Royce.

You say, "Which one gets the most for the money?" That depends upon how much money you have; nevertheless, it's a good question. On a square foot basis, the VW bug costs less. On a comfort basis, you get a lot for the money with a Rolls.

Carry the car analogy another step. Architects generally agree that if you have the money to buy a Pontiac building (or a Mercury or some other middle-class category), you can get a beautiful, efficient building or an ugly, inefficient one for the same amount of money. In other words, good design isn't an extra; sometimes it even costs less.

Some architects like the "lean and clean" look.

They have a taste for buildings that are free of the superfluous. They love economy—maximum effect with minimum means. Their clients love economy because it's easy on their pocketbooks. Now that conservation of nature and conservation of energy have taken to the center stage, the public has begun to accept the esthetics of economy. There's a new meaning to "less is more." There is beauty in efficiency.

If you understand the igloo (an ingeniously developed way of constructing an energy-efficient shelter), you appreciate it. If you understand the wigwam (an ingeniously developed mobile home with an innovative method of natural ventilation), you appreciate it. Just because something costs a lot of money doesn't make it beautiful. There are overdressed buildings just as there are overdressed people. True, exaggeration and exhibitionism are major design concepts. However, there is dignity of restraint in many great buildings. The simple way of doing things, architecturally speaking, is generally the best and the most visually acceptable way.

Wherever form has an understandable function, there is maximum appreciation. Take architects George Nelson and Charles Eames, who designed early classic Herman Miller furniture, for example. They played a strong part in creating the esthetics of economy. Furniture is small enough to understand. Just about every part can be seen. In the case of their furniture, every form has a function. It is beautifully composed and proportioned. There is beauty in the machine finishes and in the new shapes that only industrialized processes can produce. Why can't a building be like an Eames chair?

The house is furniture to live in; the city is a big house.

Many architects are emulating this philosophy—that through industrialization, using new technology and new materials, the masses can afford simple, beautiful buildings that reflect the spirit of a new era.

Above: If it works, is it beautiful? Not necessarily. Conversely, if it doesn't work, is it ugly? It probably is, to the user. Efficiency does not guarantee beauty, but it certainly increases appreciation.

Look at this photo of the DeVry Institute in Chicago. At first, you probably won't classify the building as beautiful. It's more likely to be seen as on the strange side. You wonder what all those steel joists are doing up there. On a beauty scale of 0 to 10, you might rate it 4, at the most. If you could study the building at the site and talk with its users, you'd learn these things: It works with the precision of a watch. There's circulation efficiency with it. Ample lighting for close work. Places to relax. Labs conducive to learning. The exposed joists permit the building to grow economically. It has a unique system for an inevitable expansion program. It was built with minimum on-site labor and in record time. It reflects the spirit of the times. There's a new esthetic relating to industrialized building systems. The users love it. The owners got a lot for their money. With this knowledge, you begin to appreciate the building more. You find you can't look at this building the same way you would look at a grand old state capitol. Now could you rate the building 8 on the beauty scale? Knowledge helps to increase appreciation, if there is something to appreciate.

Above: Another strange building, yet completely different. At first glance it might not rate much on your beauty scale either. However, to some people who are familiar with air-supported roofs, a first glance would rate it high. These people know that the building represents a new, economical way of spanning large spaces. They know that this building could not have been built 10 years ago, that it represents the most advanced technology, and that it is one of the first permanent air-supported structures. They know that the cost is relatively low—much less than a steel or concrete facility. What they probably appreciate the most about this building is: it will be the granddaddy of super air-supported structures which someday may cover a large city downtown area or an entire small city. What does knowing this do to your appreciation? Does the building look better?

The "dog trots" (or possum runs) of the last century provided southern comfort living during the hot months. The living units on each side cause a venturi effect with the cooling breeze. Use of this type of breezeway in hot, humid climates makes sense in this day of energy shortage. And a breeze created by electricity from a power plant can't match the quality of nature's cool summer breeze. Architects should know how wind behaves in and around buildings. Knowledge of the wind saves energy. This 1824–1836 Texas house might serve as a model for an energy-conserving house for the 1980s.

ENERGY

If a building burns excessive energy to make it run, it's not a successful building. The energy consideration is becoming increasingly important as the oil and gas wells run dry. Your grandfather (and your great grandfather) thought the pot-bellied stove was "the cat's meow"—a thing of beauty, the epitome of efficiency. Then came central heating. Next to sliced bread, central heating was the greatest technological advancement of the century. But grandmother still had to cook on a cast-iron stove with wood and coal.

Senior citizens from the Midwest remember their childhoods—having to get up early to start the fires with corn cobs which were hauled in by horse and wagon and dumped in the backyard. These children of the 20s vividly recall the lumps on their heads from the inevitable corn cob fights among the children of the neighborhood. Grandmother had it worse. Dirty, unreliable cooking heat saw to that.

Then progress brought cooking with gas ("cooking with gas" still lingers as an expression of progress) and electricity. Out went the corn cobs. In came the high cost of cooking with gas. Comparatively, very expensive in the 30s and 40s and extending to the mid-50s. Architects were cost-conscious, fully aware of the cost of energy to run a

uilding. They designed buildings
at conserved energy and saved
perational cost.

**Vhatever lessons architects
earned about economy in the
0s, they forgot in the 60s.**

orm became arbitrary. Saving fuel
asn't a consideration. Formalism
revailed. The architect asked the
ollaborating engineer if it was fea-
ble to put an all-glass wall on the
est. ''Sure,'' he said, ''I can make
ou comfy—winter or summer. You
on't even need overhangs or sun
affles. Make the building all glass if
ou want to. There's plenty of cheap
nergy.''

The photograph below is of a cold weather
building; the photo on the left of a hot weather
building. Although these two were built a
century apart, both were designed using
fundamentals of climate control relating to
orientation, fenestration, climate benefits,
and climate detriments. When architects
acknowledge nature, energy is saved.

All-glass buildings appeared everywhere, disregarding sun, wind, heat, and cold. Ignoring orientation. Mindless of the economy of insulation. Violating rules of fenestration keep buildings warm in winter and cool in summer. Rational planning disappeared. Regionalism faded. Buildings in Alaska began to look like buildings in Florida. Why not? Technology was available. All it took was cheap fuel. Plenty of that around then.

In the affluent 60s, conservation of energy wasn't even discussed during the design process. In the 70s, it's another story. A real energy shortage. Fuel costs tripled. Now those 60s buildings are burning up energy which will become even more scarce and more expensive. Cheap energy has gone the way of the buffalo.

Energy conservation as a design determinant will be the name of the game from now on. Energy conservation could have much more impact on building design than the great "form-givers" of the last three decades—architects like Le Corbusier, Mies, Gropius, and Kahn.

Energy will be the new form-giver.

Buildings now consume about one third of all the energy used in this country. Half of that could be saved if buildings were properly designed. How to save 50 percent of the energy wasted? By solar energy? There's a fallacy in thinking solar energy is the answer for curing the ills of heat-leaking buildings. At this time in history, solar energy is an expensive substitute for fossil fuels. Solar energy cannot now, and will not in the near future, solve the energy shortage. But 50 percent wasted energy can be saved simply through better design.

Solar energy will help, but not as much as proponents have led us to believe. What's good about a solar-heated building if the heat leaks out? The sun can't make up for bad buildings. Solar heating in particular requires energy-efficient buildings.

To ignore the sun is folly. It should be put to work. And it has been. People have always used the sun. Basking in the sun to keep warm. Drying food. Curing animal skins. Baking bricks. Orienting dwellings to receive the warming winter sun.

And making openings away from the cold wintry winds.

Advanced technology can convert sun rays into electricity. Doing it economically is still a thing of the future. But there are other ways the sun can help on a sophisticated level.

Here are four basic ways to put the sun to work:

Sun to Space: Put glass where you want the sun to enter the building so as to heat the inside surfaces which heat the space which warms the body—the "greenhouse effect." Been used for ages.

Sun to Mass: Use a sun-heated sustaining wall (or roof or pool of water) to transfer heat inside to warm the air which warms the body by conduction and radiation. Been used for ages.

Sun to Collector: Use a solar collector to heat water (or air) and store it for distribution when needed to heat the space which warms the body (or cools the body by absorption—still expensive). Relatively new.

Sun to Solar Cell: Use a solar cell to convert solar energy into electrical energy for storage until needed to heat or to cool the body. Very expensive.

The last way is too expensive for general use. But wait a decade or two. By then solar energy will help significantly to relieve the energy shortage, maybe supplying as much as 10 percent of the energy used for all buildings. This can happen only if the government continues to sponsor the sun.

Much can be done today if architects would do it. Through design, architects can reduce the energy required to run buildings regardless of what fuel is used. All they have to do is get back on the economy track.

The cost of energy is going to get higher. Money shapes buildings. Energy is money. So energy shapes buildings. It's as simple as that.

But energy costs more than money. Think about this: One large building can cause the destruction of a forest, just for the electricity it

Pages 138–139: Keeping the sun off the glass will cut your air-conditioning bill as much as 25 percent.

will use. Or it can ruin a beautiful view of meadows and rolling hills, stripped and scarred by mining for solid energy. Or it can permanently mar a beautiful seascape to bring liquid energy to the surface. It would be hard to appreciate that particular building.

The sin of sins will be to design obese buildings having insatiable appetites for consuming energy.

No longer can architects design fat, excessive energy-consuming, energy-leaking buildings. Regardless of what energy is used—natural gas, Arabian oil, Alaskan oil, North Sea oil, Mexican oil, Texas oil, Colorado shale, West Virginia coal, nuclear energy, hot liquids from the earth, the tides, the wind, the sun, or whale oil—architects are beginning to return to fundamentals of orientation and fenestration. They know that the underlying principle of design is:

Function, form, economy, and time are one.

Buildings must be lean and clean. They must be efficient, having economical space and form. They must run on minimum energy. They must be for tomorrow as well as today. No other alternative. There is an increasing demand by the public for energy-efficient buildings.

How does this relate to architecture appreciation? Buildings that guzzle energy become hard to appreciate. Conversely, buildings designed with emphasis on energy conservation are easy to appreciate. For some time to come, energy efficiency will be among the evaluative criteria for judging buildings by professionals and laypeople.

What makes an energy-efficient building? The following considerations:

Proper Orientation: Architects and engineers with computers can establish the actual orientation of a building for minimum use of energy. If 360 different orientations were calculated, fuel consumption would vary as much as 25 percent.

Daylighting: It's free. It saves electricity, provided glass is used judiciously.

Sun Controls: Overhangs, sun baffles, and outside blinds reduce cool-

Opposite page, top: A paradox that architects seem to have is whether to keep glass areas to a minimum and conserve energy or use glass liberally for a magnificent view. But it's not as much a paradox as you might expect. A lot depends on climate, exposure, kind of glass, how it's protected from the sun, and many other factors. Consider this example. The dramatic view is from a hotel room in Honolulu. Winter heat loss is not a problem. Controlling the sun is. The solution: over-hangs and baffles. Were this building located in a cold climate, double glazing or minimum glass might be used. Architects must determine judicious use of glass for each situation.

Opposite page, bottom: Admitting the sun on cold days saves heating cost. The sun doesn't directly warm the air; it warms the interior surfaces which warm the air by conduction. A person in sunlight is warmed by radiation. In a situation like this, if the outside temperature were freezing, the two people probably would not need any heat. It's the "greenhouse effect."

Left: Here are three basic sun controls. For southern exposure, the "overhang" (top) is best. For southeast and southwest, the "box" (middle) is best. And for east and west exposures, "baffles" (bottom) are the most effective.

ing loads by 20 to 25 percent. During winter months, if controls permit sun to enter through the windows, rooms with southern exposure can be heated during the day in freezing weather by the sun alone.

Regionalism: Buildings tailored for specific climates are energy-savers. A building design for Massachusetts should not be built in Louisiana or vice versa. It is an affront to energy conservation.

No Waste Space: The more space there is, the more energy required. Most buildings have too much area. Many could have their area reduced by one-third without sacrificing function or amenities. That cuts the heating and cooling bill by one third.

Outdoor Spaces: The use of conditioned outdoor spaces—patios, cloisters and courts—saves energy. The plantation houses with peripheral porches save energy. Thomas Jefferson's use of outdoor corridors in Monticello and the University of Virginia reflects his concern for energy efficiency. The colonnade was an invention of necessity related to minimizing heated space. Why heat the halls?

Geometry: Two buildings with the same floor area and the same materials but different geometry could vary as much as 20 percent in energy requirements. The Eskimos knew what they were doing when they made the igloo. A circular plan has the most floor area for the least perimeter. The more compact, the better. Too many zigzags on the floor plan increase energy consumption.

A new morality of form is emerging.

The next decade will bring new forms based on this new energy morality. An indignant public will see to that. People won't tolerate buildings which leak energy. They will demand efficiencies in their buildings just as they are demanding efficiencies in their cars. The era of cheap energy has ended and appreciation of energy-saving buildings has begun.

Opposite page: This building group at Harvard University in Cambridge, Massachusetts (top, background), wears an Ivy League tweed coat (original Harvard brick) because of the cold climate. The California counterpart—the Four College Science Building at Claremont College (bottom)—wears short sleeves. Corridors and some "classrooms" are designed as conditioned outdoor spaces. Each is indigenous.

Top and middle: Keep heated and air-conditioned areas to a minimum—that's the best way to save energy. In other words, it's a lot more energy efficient to have outdoor corridors, colonnades, porches, and protected patios than to have these spaces heated and cooled. Because such spaces usually have protective roofs and walls, architects refer to them as "conditioned outdoor spaces." In the winter they serve as windbreaks and sun pockets; in the summer they provide shade and natural cross ventilation. Often the strongest architectural feeling occurs in these protected areas. It's like the beach—the overlap of two realms (land and water). A porch is the beach of two worlds (inside and outside).

Bottom: Thomas Jefferson knew how to save energy. When he designed the University of Virginia, he must have had the pragmatic thought, "Why heat the halls?" Perhaps this is why he made so much use of outdoor corridors.

10. Time Quality

To fully appreciate a building, you should know when it was built. Learn if it was a pacesetter in its time. That is particularly important to know. The pacesetters deserve special attention, greater appreciation.

There are three aspects of time relating to a building. The first is when the building was built. A good architectural historian can determine this simply by looking. If it was built in the last four decades, he can zero in on the exact year. This time-quality applies to every building in every period of history. If a building was built centuries ago, a historian can give the century. So can you with a little study.

You hear people refer to a building as having a timeless quality. Some buildings, like people, seem to defy time. The fact is:

Buildings have a time-quality, not a timeless quality.

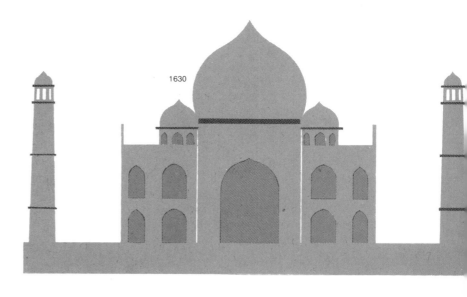

1630

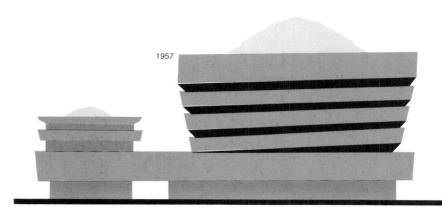

1957

What you see in this vista is a contrast in time. Each building tells the story of its time. Although they do this in completely different technological languages, the two messages come across in clear, simple expressions.

A second aspect of time relates to function. Time changes lifestyles, resulting in change of building function. When function changes, so does form through modifications or expansions. A building, in a sense, is never completed. The ancient Egyptian temple at Karnak grew for 2,000 years. Many cathedrals took over a century to build and were used during construction. Buildings seem to always need modifications. Modifications were made continuously on the Louvre from the Middle Ages to the 19th century. The U.S. capitol in Washington, the work of several architects, has had continual modifications and additions from its very beginning in 1793 when President George Washington set the cornerstone. A private, single-family residence has had seven additions in 20 years, not to mention the many modifications of existing spaces.

A building is never completed.

The third aspect relates to the time a person experiences the building. More often than not, one has a different value system today than he did 10 years ago. The beautiful glass highrises built in the 60s, for example, may not look so pretty in the 80s to the person who knows they guzzle excessive energy.

Time changes a person. Time changes his sensitivity and response to space and form. The Ronchamp Chapel, designed by Le Corbusier, is a case in point. At first most people disliked it. One architect expressed the consensus, ''It left me cold.'' He was repelled by the building's strangeness and by its seemingly irrational form. Five years

LINEAR GROWTH

ORGANIC GROWTH

later, this same architect said, "I studied the logic of this chapel and gradually I became empathetic to its form and space. Now this building has a spiritual aura I had never before experienced." The "intellectual being" of this architect changed during the 5-year period. His architectural experience was enriched by new knowledge—knowledge acquired slowly over that period of time. Time made the architect different. Time makes you different.

There's a good chance that 5 years ago you experienced a building for the first time and were impressed by its new, exciting space and form. Today, however, the building is a bore. What happened? The building is the same as it was when you first saw it. It hasn't changed. You have. You have a different value system. A person can change drastically in 5 years.

Are you wearing the same kind of clothes you were wearing 5 years ago? The same hairstyle? Do you watch the same kind of TV programs you did then? Are you reading the same kind of books? Has travel changed your values? You look at a familiar building. You say, "That is old hat. Where are the innovations?" You expect new stimuli. Or it might well be that during the 5-year period you developed more knowledge of the building. It's *when* you experience space and form that counts.

Time changes your responses

Top and middle: Most people prefer a "feeling of completeness" at every stage of development of a building. They don't want it to look unfinished. There are a few people, however, who like an "esthetics of incompleteness" because they feel that no building is finished. Here are examples of buildings deliberately designed to look incomplete, to look young, capable of growing without growing pains.

Bottom: Construction of the Palais du Louvre of Paris continued from the time of Francis I (1546) through Napoleon III (1878). You can imagine the number of architects involved and how the facades and rooms changed to meet the whims of each architect, if not the ruling owners.

Right: When Le Corbusier's chapel in Ronchamp, Haute Saone, France, first appeared in the architectural journals, his devoted disciples were shocked and confused. They acted as if their god had betrayed them. One said, "Why did he forsake logic? Why did he switch to pure sculpture? Why did he discard everything he taught us? I feel like I've been double-crossed." But this little chapel is a masterpiece of curvilinear plastic form, with a very subtle planar effect caused by the detached roof and walls. It epitomizes the high art of daylighting. It came at a time when there was a need for a breakaway from solid, stifling, rectilinear spaces and forms. Unquestionably the chapel in Ronchamps was a new kind of building which appeared at exactly the right time in architectural history.

It shocked people, that's for sure. But only the uninformed. Actually, it doesn't take much study to hone your appreciation. Buildings are not all that difficult to understand.

Below: The Tremaine House in Santa Barbara, California, was designed by Richard Neutra, who was responsible for many superb buildings during the 30s and 40s. When it was built, it was a source of inspiration to those few architects at that time who searched for logic of form and the fluid quality of space. To others it was a revelation—to see industrialized form be given human qualities.

Right: Wright's Guggenheim Museum in New York, a controversy from its conception, is a building with a sustaining quality that is sure to bring enjoyment to future generations. As one visitor remarked, ''It's something you won't forget.'' That's a good characteristic for any building. Or anyone. Who wants to be forgotten?

Below: Why do certain people never seem to grow old? Perhaps because they have kept up with the times or are ahead. The same with buildings. The Robie House in Chicago, with its daring ''new'' cantilever forms, came into the architectural world in 1909. It's still ahead of the times, an architectural masterpiece. This is one of Frank Lloyd Wright's best works and evidence that he was a truly great artistic innovator.

Opposite page: People who visit Moscow leave with an indelible memory of St. Basil. It's an amazing building inside and out. Architects would call the plan ''the mother hen and little chickens'' composition—one large church surrounded by eight small ones. It was built by Ivan the Terrible in the 16th century to commemorate his victories. The exterior is fantastic; there is no other word for it. Characteristically Russian, it has onion domes, but these are variegated with many bright colors. There can be no better termination of the vista at one end of Red Square than St. Basil. If ''buildings are pages of history,'' this one deserves a double spread. It's seen a lot of history.

SUSTAINING CHARACTER

Some buildings have an explicit, sustaining quality. Frank Lloyd Wright's innovative, skillfully designed houses have that quality. Think back. Don't certain houses in the neighborhood where you live or once lived have that quality? A few churches too? There always seems to be at least one building on every university campus that possesses a sustaining quality.

Go further back into history. The Acropolis in Athens not only endured the ravages of nature and man's destruction, but managed to live through the ages, epitomizing the consummation of masonry and sculpture—pure beauty. The Colosseum in Rome has another kind of sustaining quality. Santa Sophia in Istanbul, still another kind. St. Mark's in Venice has this sustaining quality too. So does Moscow's St. Basil. And Sir Christopher Wren's churches. The list is long. Every historical style has its masterpieces—buildings with a sustaining quality.

The list gets even longer when you include the masterwork of vernacular buildings—the enduring adobe and stone pueblos of the Southwest and Mexico, the barns of New England, and the grain storage structures of the Middle West. These seem to have that "timeless quality" that everybody talks about. More accurately stated, they have a sustaining quality.

A building has a sustaining quality when people still like it after years or even centuries. Take the Taj Mahal—it was modern in its time, incorporating the most advanced methods of design, technology, and craftsmanship of the period. Those methods are obsolete today; yet the building has sustained the quality that can create architecture for most people. Modern-day architects are thrilled when they experience its space and form.

Great buildings have a sustaining quality whether they are 5 months, 5 years, or 5 centuries old.

That's why they are great. They are the best of their time. More often they are the pacesetters. They possess a sustaining quality of space and form. Lasting vitality is a distinguishing mark of a great building.

HISTORY

"Buildings are pages of history." That's a notion the average person finds a bit farfetched. Egyptian temples may seem rather remote, hidden in the blowing sands of time. The United Nations building may seem a bit closer. What about buildings being pages of your own personal history? The building in which you were born? The dwelling you remember as a youngster? Your elementary school? Your high school? Your favorite college building? Your current residence? They speak clearly about you. To find out who you are, look at your living room or study.

Buildings reflect the development of people—their culture, technological advances, hopes, and aspirations. Each individual has a personal choice. The space in which you live reflects *you*, specifically your values. It's that way with nations too.

Buildings mirror lifestyles, economics, and technology of their time.

Buildings relate to how people prefer to live, work, play, learn, and believe. Gothic cathedrals reflect the heady moral and religious values of their particular era as well as the technological developments which made tall stone structures possible. Scottish castles show, in no uncertain terms, the warlike period of the time and the functional innovation of the architects. Skyscrapers represent the economic values of the modern era as well as its technological advances, specifically the invention of the elevator and steel-frame construction.

Pages 150–151: Buildings change with the time. So do the notions of beauty because society, individuals, speed, duty, morals, and culture change. What looks good to one generation doesn't set so well with another. The educated person, however, has deep appreciation for the best buildings of each historical period.

The long history of buildings in England, France, Spain, Italy, Russia, India, Turkey and Greece, to name a few, far surpasses that of buildings in the U.S. Our short history is another matter. In only two centuries this country has become rich with quality buildings. Every region has its own unique, abundantly impressive architectural heritage. Almost every city has fine old buildings which characterize the lifestyles of the specific periods in which they were built. You can look at these buildings and, without entering, tell what kind of clothes the users wore, what kind of vehicles they rode in, and what kind of furniture and furnishings they used. Did you ever notice how buildings, furniture, and clothes of a specific period seem to look alike?

Look around you in your own city. Every city has buildings of historical significance. Contact the local preservation groups and architectural heritage societies. Find out when tours are conducted through these wonderful old arks. It'll be worth your trouble to experience their space and form. Any knowledge of the history of old buildings helps to enrich the architectural experience of new ones.

Humans build. What they build is telling evidence of the values of society. How they build depends upon the extent of technology.

The present reflects the past. What people build reveals their values. How they build tells the explicitness of their technology. Obviously this building is of this generation. It could not have been built when your grandfather was your age. The technology of structure at that time would not have permitted the giant cantilevers. Technology of materials had not produced the insulative, low-brightness glass. It's a building that expresses its own time. Technology helps do it.

TECHNOLOGY

The word "technology" has been mentioned quite a few times in this book. Let's dwell some more on it here. The technology of buildings concerns systems (structural, heating, air-conditioning, electrical, elevator and escalator, and many more), materials, and methods of construction. Think of technology as related to providing comfort, as the way in which materials are made and put together. Technology helps shape buildings. It always has. Most probably it will continue to. The technology of each era establishes the width and height of columnless space. The ancient Egyptians' technology permitted high structures but not large spans. Cheops, the biggest of the pyramids, was 481 feet (145 m) high before the polished limestone apex was effaced. It's still a mystery how the huge stones, averaging 2.5 tons (some weighed 200 tons), were placed in perfect alignment at such heights. The Karnak Temple (still standing after more than 2,500 years) has stone columns six stories high. Another mystery: How did the builders place those boulders nearly 70 feet (22 m) in the air? With all their knowledge about how to build high, their technology limited going wide—the span between columns could only equal the width of the stone roof slabs. Today's technology permits enormous spans. The Karnak Temple took centuries to build. Institutions larger in floor area than Karnak can be constructed in less than three years.

Technology concerns process as well as product. Technology determines what materials are used and how. Technology creates form. Technology is the logic of form. It helps provide the spirit of form. Technology ties form to time. There can be no new forms—new sizes, new shapes, new materials—unless technology permits. Today architects and engineers need not ape old styles. Technology allows them almost unlimited opportunities to develop new forms. How ridiculous to imitate forms of other ages. The Gothic forms belong to their age of technology, not ours. A Tudor house, transposed to the 20th century and set in the middle of a Kansas prairie, is out of time and out of place.

There is one old ark which contin-
ues to thrill its users and visitors, the Bradbury Building, in Los Angeles. Built around the turn of the century, it was very modern when the users moved in. Cast iron is the predominant material. This fine building represented the logic and spirit of the Industrial Age—the best that technology had to offer then. It was practical because the prefabricated parts could be turned out economically through mass production in the factory. The skeletal form is real. And still beautiful. This building is no copy. It had its own place and time in history. It's still hanging in there as a working building and pleasing its users. Still beautiful—very beautiful to the knowledgeable person. It possesses a sustaining quality.

It's unlikely that another building like this one will ever be built—the prefab cast iron structural elements are no longer available. Someone, however, will try to reproduce the elements in plaster or plastic! Modern technology allows any "style" to be reproduced. But not real style. During World War II "maraschino cherries" were produced from edible paper. Plastic "cast-iron elements" are even harder to accept.

Why architects even try to copy the past is beyond comprehension. They should know what they produce will be mere trappings of another era—only skin-deep. Technology goes deeper. Technology gets right down to the individual's physical, emotional, and intellectual comfort.

Comfort goes beyond the physical. Minor flaws—like a temperature crack in the wall, an uneven floor, peeling paint—are major distractions on physical, emotional, and intellectual levels. Had these flaws been prevented by better technology, the building would be better appreciated.

Comfort depends upon technology.

Right: Technology changes lifestyles. Look what the car did. It changed the city. Look what welding did to sculpture. It changed art. Look what disks and tapes did. They changed music. Even more dramatic is what technology has done and will continue to do to buildings. Top is the University of Santa Clara Activity Center—an air-supported roof structure. Air-supported buildings offer savings in time and money required for construction; they provide quality daylighting; and they are very economical for enveloping large areas. Count on more of these. Compare this building with the one below. Contrastingly different. One is light and airy; the other heavy with great visual strength.

The bottom view is the lobby of the Thomas Hall for the Performing Arts in Akron, Ohio. The mobile sculpture is not just hanging there, it works. It serves as weights, like the old-fashioned window sash weights that once were hidden in the jambs of double-hung windows. These weights allow the ceiling of the house to be raised and lowered to change the physical and acoustical volume. When the ceiling is moved, the sculpture changes—a harmonious marriage of art and technology. Appreciation is greatly intensified when you understand technology.

Opposite page: The Bradbury Building in Los Angeles, constructed at the turn of the century, is a product of the Industrial Age. That was the time of the masters of cast iron. You might say the architects were masters of space and of daylighting too. Iron technology more than anything else reveals the age of this building.

Esthetics relate to comfort. A building can be efficiently arranged, beautifully proportioned, and superbly made of the best materials, but if the user is uncomfortable—too hot or too cold—his appreciation dips as the temperature dips or rises. When there's too little lighting or too much glare, appreciation suffers. If the user can't hear the cellos at a concert, more suffering. If the elevators are too slow, no one likes the building. A stopped-up, gold water-closet is less appreciated than a clay one that works. If the roof leaks and your antique oriental rug gets wet, appreciation suffers. If *you* get wet, it suffers more.

A frantic client once called Frank Lloyd Wright late one rainy night to ask what she should do about a leak in her living room. Charismatic Wright allegedly replied, ''Put a bucket under it.'' Dodging dripping water doesn't enhance the architectural experience, that's for sure—even for a Wright masterpiece.

Since 1950 there has been a curious change in esthetics relating to technology. Back then most people abhorred the sight of heating ducts, steel trusses, beams, and joists. Today they don't like these components to be hidden. The growing desire to see components expressed sculpturally has led architects to design the various systems into one integrated, colorful system, exposed to view. The passageway (top) over a major downtown Houston street, from an office building to a hotel, frankly exposes the connecting utility services and the structural elements. It's done in an artistic manner. Most people enjoy it—it's like walking through giant sculpture.

This school (right) is an example of an integrated system. The children experience the positive aspects of modern technology. Central heating and air conditioning make them comfortable all year long. They see how it's done. The exposed integrated mechanical, electrical, and structural systems give them a daily lesson in building anatomy. They like the visual excitement. Technology enriches their daily lives.

11. Design

To fully appreciate a building, it helps to know about the process of design—what the architect does.

Designing a building is not unlike designing a chair. The first thing is to find out what the problem is.

That's called "programming," often referred to by the profession as problem seeking. Obviously to program a chair is much simpler than to program a large, complex building, which sometimes requires computers to help organize and simplify the many aspects and nuances of functional and social requirements.

So problem seeking is the first step in the total design process. The second step is problem solving— that phase relates to conceptual design. The third step, design development, is concerned with the details. The fourth step relates to finishing the contractual drawings—blueprints. The fifth step, obviously, is to construct the building.

Designing a building is no simple task. To arrive at a strong, simple solution generally requires scores of diagrammatic analyses relating to function, form, economy, and time considerations; hundreds of tracing paper studies and many of models— depending upon the character and size of the building. Design is the search for rightness. Design proceeds from complexity to simplicity. Design concerns fulfilling human needs. Design requires creativity. Design is many things, but the underlying task of design is this:

Design reconciles function, form, economy, and time.

When these four forces which shape a building are in successful balance, architecture has a better chance of happening. Nothing new. Vitruvius said about the same thing using words like "commodity, firmness and delight." Design has always been a juggling act. This is where creativity comes in. Only those architects who are endowed with both logic and creativity find the balance.

Design is solving problems; creativity achieves original solutions. Such solutions are intriguing and appealing to your desire for diversity—contrasted with the appeal of security in a familiar solution. Sometimes original solutions are so iconoclastic that it may take some time before their validity is proven. It is very much like the initial rejection of the Impressionists' paintings which became so popular later on. Strange, repelling buildings may become appealing in time.

To fully appreciate a building, it helps too to know something about architects. They are admittedly a strange breed. Most creative people are a bit strange at times. Architects seem to thrive on change. One decade they go in one direction; the next decade they do a complete turnaround and go in the opposite direction. This is not all bad. They are searching for new and meaningful forms, more economical solutions, buildings that function better and are timely. Sometimes architects have to go back to pick up good things that were left behind. That's human.

In the late 40s an old architect remarked, "It wouldn't surprise me if one day we'll be doing 'punched hole windows' again." He said this when "ribbon windows" were in style. A young architect heard him and retorted, "That old bastard can't see beyond the end of his nose. 'Punch holes' will never return." He was right—for about a decade. By then the ribbon window had grown so much that it ate up all the wall, leaving only a frame and glass—a pure Miesian effect.

The turn-around came. The punched hole in the solid wall returned! Architects forsook the ribbon window. A decade later (the late 70s) another turnaround occurred. The ribbon window returned, as popular as it was in the early 50s. The reason? Saving energy? Or was it that the architects wanted to do something different? Probably both.

Like aviators, architects love to make 180° turns. Most often they turn for good reasons. Changes in technology, economy, and lifestyle demand it.

Architects in the early 50s were functionalists obsessed with making things work. "If it works, it'll look good." They adopted Louis Sullivan's famous dictum: "Form follows function."

Then the turnaround.

Proteus-like, they changed. Architects became formalists—obsessed with creating beautiful form. "If it looks good, the people will be happy." Using "universal space" that can be adapted to any function was the rationale. Their 1960s maxim: "Function follows form."

In the 70s architects returned to the function emphasis. They talked about performance. Attended seminars on how to measure performance. On life-cycle cost. Because of a declining economy, they searched for ways "to cut out the fat" (waste space) in order to cut cost. They searched for better planning techniques to make sure buildings would perform with a high degree of efficiency. They are still trying to produce better buildings.

During the 50s architects loved lightness. They used the expression "floating architecture." The load-bearing wall became an anachronism. They liked buildings to appear to be suspended in air, hovering above the ground instead of dug in. Lightness was goodness.

A decade later came the turnaround. Advancements in concrete technology helped bring on the change. In the 60s architects went from lightness to heaviness. They wanted permanent-looking buildings. Not those light ones that looked like they would not last beyond the amortization period.

They rediscovered monumentality. Some reinvented the arch. Award juries gave prizes to the heavies, as if they had weighed each submission.

A decade later in the 70s, architects made another 180° turn. Lightness came back in vogue. Glass and metal walls replaced concrete and brick. They had expressions: "elegant lightness," "machine esthetics," "the crystalline effect," "the building system look."

And so it goes.

In fairness to architects it should be pointed out that this seemingly erratic behavior is necessary if the art and science of building design is to advance. There must always be pacesetting buildings, incorporating new ideas, new materials, and new construction methods. There must be buildings that people can afford.

When new ideas, resulting in a new form, appear upon the scene, the public is usually shocked.

Suspend your judgment until you acquire more knowledge. Ask yourself questions: What caused the change? New technology? New lifestyle requiring a new functional response by the building? New way to express the spirit of the times? Or simply a better and more creative way of solving old problems?

That's why it's important for you to have an open mind and a willingness to study new buildings that at first seem strange. When you accumulate more knowledge of buildings—new and old—and raise your level of appreciation, you will be fascinated to observe the way architects change their ways of design, even their vernacular relating to new lifestyles, new technology, economic trends, new sociological emphases, and new philosophical thought. There are literally thousands of forces that shape buildings. Architects try to be attuned and responsive to these forces. Architects are important to the economic and cultural growth of the nation—but this is not a commercial. Architects are not as important as architecture.

Buildings without architecture are like a world without art or music—not a very nice place to live.

Pages 159–161: Buildings are like people. Some are very physical, like a young man on a beach flexing his muscles. Some are overemotional, with excessive sentimentality that deliberately preys on the emotions of the observer. Some are deeply intellectual. Some look dumb and are not very smart about taking care of users efficiently and effectively. A well-known professor of architecture, when criticizing a student's design which lacked functional and structural significance, but had a certain glamorous appearance, said, "Jones, your solution is all sex and no substance." Buildings are anthropomorphic. They appear masculine or feminine. Loud or quiet. Nervous or calm. Gaudy or restrained. Frivolous or serious. Fat or lean. Friendly or distant. Poor or rich. Stately or stodgy. When you look at these buildings, use your own terms. At first the exercise may appear a bit silly, but it's a good bet you will have more insight about buildings from the experience. You'll discover one is very physical, another has imagination with no substance, while at least two are highly imaginative with substance. Do you find one has a stately quality? Is it strange? Or quaint? Let yourself go. You are the final judge. You are always the final judge. Only you know whether a building possesses architecture—for you.

12. Wrap-up

That's it for the basics of architecture appreciation. In a nutshell, here's what it's all about:

Architecture is a personal, enjoyable, necessary experience.

Buildings are for people to enjoy. The most important thing any specific building can do is respond to human needs—physical, emotional, and intellectual.

A building is made up of space and form. There are two kinds of space—static and dynamic. And three kinds of form—plastic, planar, skeletal.

History tells much about what buildings do, how successfully they have functioned.

The historical styles warrant study. Remember, there is a great difference between real historical styles and the labels found in real estate ads. It's the difference between style and "style." Style mirrors the culture when it was built. "Style" mocks.

A building has a time quality. Knowledgeable observers can tell how old a building is.

The search for eye-pleasing proportion is never ending. Technology helps determine what seems right. So does scale. The language of architects, critics, and historians includes scores of different scales. Each will fall into one of three categories—physical, associative, and effectual.

Composing space and form artistically into meaningful and beautiful total-form requires great skill. Architects are not all alike. Some have greater compositional skills than others. Their buildings show it.

Buildings relate to societal needs. Buildings are the fulfillment of these needs. A nation's buildings reflect its social goals.

In the psychological sense, buildings help or hinder.

The rules of color relate to the experience and perception of the person who experiences the color.

Light is the architect's medium as much as brick and steel.

Great buildings have a sustaining quality.

How a building grows and develops is a strong consideration because most buildings grow. If not, certainly they are refitted for change of function and efficiency.

There can be no new forms and greater spaces unless technology permits.

Excellent buildings must have the architect's love and tender care from the mass to the smallest detail.

The ground and sky connections—where building meets earth and sky—are the most important connections.

If the design of the small connections is skillfully handled, there's a good chance that the building will be a good one. Details reveal architects' competence as much as anything.

There has always been symbolism. Some buildings are themselves symbols.

Architects search for simple, clear expressions in space and form, although at times complexity and ambiguity have been admired and designed into buildings either consciously or subconsciously.

Energy conservation is a design determinant. It may be the new form-giver.

A successful building achieves a successful balance of function, form, economy, and time.

You are the final judge as to whether a specific building possesses architecture.

In the case of a building having design excellence, the more you know about the building the more intense will be your architecture experience.

With more knowledge there is deeper appreciation which provides more enjoyment.

Glossary of Terms and List of Architects

TERMS

This is not a dictionary of architecture. It is simply a glossary of words used in this book and by architects, sometimes with a special meaning in mind.

Air distribution That part of an air-conditioning or mechanical ventilation system which controls the distribution of air.

Air-supported structure A structure, generally the roof, made of fabric anchored down, sealed at its perimeter, and inflated with a steady introduction of air that maintains a pressure of approximately 5 pounds per square foot.

Arch A form of masonry construction, such as brick and stone, used to span an opening in a wall. An arch is self-supporting and will support weight imposed on it by carrying the downward thrust first laterally and then downward to the vertical supports

Asymmetry Lack of symmetry, but possibly with axial balance.

Balloon framing The type of wood framing in which the vertical members (studs) extend from the foundation to the roof in one continuous piece without a break for second floor joists. (In western framing, the studs of each floor are separate pieces, each resting on a sill.) Balloon framing seems to cause buildings under construction to "balloon up" quickly.

Bilateral lighting Daylight entering a room from two (opposite) sides that results in an even distribution of light throughout the room.

Built-up roof A comparatively flat roof made of several layers of impregnated felt, with hot tar or asphalt mopped between each layer and on the top of the last layer to receive a protective covering of pea gravel or crushed stone.

Cable suspension A tensional structure using heavy wire rope and/or a group of parallel wire ropes as structural members.

Cantilever A horizontal projection without external support that appears to defy gravity, such as a canopy or a balcony. It is actually supported by a downward force behind a wall or column that acts as a fulcrum.

Clear span The distance between the supports for a beam, truss, arch, dome, or any device which permits open space below.

Clerestory Windows in the upper part of a building that extend above the adjacent roof to admit extra light into the interior.

Climate Regional and seasonal temperatures, amounts of precipitation, percentages of humidity, sun angles, and directions of prevailing winds, all of which can influence the design of a building.

Column module Half the diameter of a classical column at the base used as a unit of measure to determine the proportions of the entire column and other parts of a

building, such as a Greek temple.

Composition The particular way in which the combination of parts in a work of art or in a building produces a harmonious whole.

Compressive stress The force per unit area due to compression of a structural member, such as a column or the leg of a chair.

Connection The meeting of two or more architectural forms or materials for a specific purpose, such as proper fit, weather tightness, added strength, or visual effectiveness.

Daylighting The admittance of natural light from the sun or sky dome into interior spaces.

Dead load The constant weight of structural materials and fixed loads used in calculating the strength of floor or roof beams and columns.

Dentil A small square block used in a series of teeth reminiscent of wood joinery ornamenting a cornice in classical architecture.

Details The connections of materials drawn in detail to describe their assembly.

Dog trot A breezeway or a covered passage between two parts of a house. Sometimes referred to as a "possum run."

Dome A roof form in the shape of a hemisphere.

Dormer A gabled window that projects from a sloping roof.

Economy The efficient use of available means for the end proposed. Implies an interest in achieving maximum results through minimum means.

Electrical distribution The routing of electrical power through wires in a conduit system to serve the lighting and power needs of the building.

Elevation The principal exterior sides of a building (front, side, and rear elevations), usually referring to approximate compass points (north elevation, south elevation, etc.). Also refers to an architectural drawing of a given side, a graphic projection upon a vertical plane at a given scale.

Envelope The enclosing skin or exterior surface of a building—walls, roofs, floors—often referred to as the fabric of a building.

Fabric See envelope.

Facade An exterior side of a building, usually the front. The front elevation or exterior face of a building.

Fenestration The arrangement of windows in a building.

Flying buttress A detached structure joined to the main wall of a Gothic church by a half arch to receive the thrust from the vault.

Free-standing Independent of an adjacent wall or other structure, as a free-standing wall or a free-standing column.

Golden section The division of a line in extreme and mean proportion. Discovered and used by the Greeks in the 5th century B.C. as pleasing proportions—for instance, the "golden" rectangle (approximately 5 x 8 inches) whose sides are in the ratio of the golden section.

Half-timber Refers to a medieval type of construction in which the structural mem-

bers are heavy timbers and the spaces between the framework are filled in with brick, plaster, or mud with straw.

Heat flow Refers to the heat loss (in winter) and heat gain (in summer) by transmission and infiltration through the building envelope.

Human needs Include such general categories as self-preservation, physical comfort, self-image, and social affiliation.

Illumination A fancy word for lighting, whether natural or electric.

Light Architects usually refer to sunlight or daylight as the light which defines form—through shades and shadows. However, it could refer to electric light.

Lintel A beam with its two ends resting upon separate supports and supporting the wall material above the opening—a window or door.

Live loads The moving load or the weight of occupants, movable furnishings, and moving vehicles on the structure.

Load-bearing wall A wall (as opposed to columns and beams) which supports the floors and roof of a building.

Mansard roof A roof having a double slope, with a steep lower slope and a flatter, shorter upper portion, creating an attic with a habitable height. Named after Francois Mansart, a French Renaissance architect.

Micro climate The climate of a specific building site as affected by adjacent buildings, landscaping, bodies of water, and topography.

Molding A strip of plain, curved, or carved wood (or other material) used to hide the uneven joint of materials or planes. Also used as a decorative device to enhance a joint or even a painting, as in the case of picture molding.

Orientation (direction) Ability to determine one's bearing or settling one's sense of direction.

Orientation (location) The location of a building with regard to the points of the compass to take advantage of climate conditions. For example, "the long axis of the building runs east and west to minimize exposure to the hot summer sun."

Parapet wall That part of an exterior wall which extends above the roof line.

Penthouse A dwelling unit built on the roof of another building. Also a mechanical room built on the roof of a building to house elevator machinery, ventilating equipment, or water tanks.

Rotunda A circular room covered by a dome.

Sawtooth roof A roof constructed with a number of trusses which has a profile similar to the teeth of a saw and permits windows to face the north light.

Symmetry Balance achieved by having identical forms or masses on either side of an axial line.

Tension stress Stress in a structural member caused by forces drawing it apart, as in a tie rod.

Three-dimension (3-D) Perceived in terms of length, width, and height.

Timber frame construction A method of building in which standard size wood structural members are used.

Topography A detailed, graphic description of a tract of land, including natural and manufactured features, showing their relative positions and elevations.

Total-form The composite form including all the elements of a building.

Trabeate style Architecture based on post and beam construction, as in Greek architecture and as distinguished from the vaulted or arched type.

Trilateral lighting Daylight entering a room from three sides—such as from windows on opposite walls and from roof skylights.

Truss A combination of straight, structural parts arranged as a triangular lacework for efficient use to span greater spaces than ordinary beams.

Unilateral lighting. Daylight entering a room from one window wall.

Venturi The effect caused by a construction of air flow between buildings close together in a microclimatic situation, which increases the velocity of air flow.

Vernacular The architecture common to a locality—indigenous and characteristic.

Windbreak Any device used to deflect the wind from its normal flow—a fence, a row of trees, or a free-standing wall designed for that specific function.

ARCHITECTS

This book is not about architects. Many are mentioned here, but only to illustrate a point in architecture appreciation. These are identified below, but do not include the many other excellent architects discussed in architectural history books and professional magazines.

Birkerts, Gunnar (b. 1925) Latvian-American architect and educator. President of Gunnar Birkerts and Associates (since 1959). Teaches at the University of Michigan (since 1961).

Principal work includes Schwartz House, Northville, Michigan (1960); Fisher Administration Center, Detroit (1966); Federal Reserve Bank of Minneapolis (1973); Tougaloo (Mississippi) College (1974); and Lincoln School, Columbus, Indiana (1970).

Breuer, Marcel (b. 1902) Hungarian-American architect and designer. Developed tubular steel furniture at the Bauhaus (the most influential school of design in the 20th century, noted for its program that synthesized technology, craftsmanship, and design esthetics) in Dessau, Germany, where Gropius was director. Best known for his originality in building design and sculptural forms. Major work includes the Whitney Museum, New York (1966); and St. John's Abbey Church and University Buildings, Collegeville, Minnesota (1967).

Brown, Denise Scott (b. 1931) American architect, educator, writer. Taught at various prestigious universities (1960–1970). Joined firm of Venturi and Rauch in Philadelphia in 1967 and became a partner in 1969. Principal work includes planning for South Central Philadelphia, U.S. Bicentennial, and The Strand, Galveston, Texas. Co-author of *Learning from Las Vegas* (1972).

Callicrates (5th century B.C.) Greek architect. Designed the Parthenon in collaboration with Ictinus.

Caudill Rowlett Scott (CRS) (founded 1946) American architectural firm. Pioneers in modern school architecture, architectural programming, and management techniques.

DaVinci, Leonardo (1452–1510) Italian artist, inventor, and architect.

Eames, Charles (b. 1907) American architect and designer. First known for his own pace-setting house in Santa Monica (1949) and his mass-produced chairs. In his creative movies and exhibits, he increases the sensuous joy of seeing with visual and verbal economy.

Franzen, Ulrich (b. 1921) German-American architect. His forceful work has a wide range of expressions, depending heavily on strong sculptural forms. Notable work includes the Alley Theatre, Houston (1969); and the Multi-categorical Research Building, Cornell University, Ithaca (1974).

Fuller, R. Buckminster (b. 1895) American inventor. Best known for his geodesic dome and his two-way trusses or "space frames."

Gropius, Walter (1883–1969) German-American architect and educator. Founder of a school of art and architecture, the famous Bauhaus (1919 Weimar, later Dessau, Germany). Great design teacher at Harvard. Pioneered an architecture for the 20th century. Practiced with a group of partners under the firm name, The Architects' Collaborative (TAC).

Ictinus (5th century B.C.) Greek architect. Designed the Parthenon in collaboration with Callicrates.

Johansen, John (b. 1916) American architect. Best known for his bold and expressive forms, the U.S. Embassy, Dublin (1964); and The Mummers Theater, Oklahoma City (1971).

Johnson, Philip (b. 1906) American architect. A student of Mies van der Rohe, he developed his own style through an impressive series of elegant buildings starting with his own glass house in New Canaan, Connecticut (1949). More recently, with partner John Burgee, he has designed such urban landmarks as the IDS Center, Minneapolis (1973), and Pennzoil Place, Houston (1976).

Kahn, Louis I. (1901–1974) American architect and educator. Sought new architectural forms based on intrinsic aspects of the design problem and on local technology. His late start began in 1951 with the Richards Medical Center in Philadelphia. Notable buildings include the Salk Institute, La Jolla, California (1965); and the Kimball Museum, Fort Worth, Texas (1972).

Le Corbusier (Charles-Edouard Jeanneret) (1887–1965) Swiss-French architect and painter. One of the pioneers of modern architecture. His early concrete buildings with egg-crate facades and elements of concrete brutality, such as the housing blocks at Marseilles (1952), influenced a generation of architects. His Pilgrimage Chapel at Ronchamp (1955) created a fu-

ror with its bold, concrete plastic forms.

Loos, Adolf (1870–1933) Czech-Austrian architect and writer. Established an anti-ornament theory and practiced it in his clean Steiner House in Vienna (1910).

Mansart, Francois (1598–1666) French architect. As a Renaissance architect of elegant country houses, he designed the mansard roof. Some two centuries later houses on the boulevards of Paris were designed with the mansard roof to sneak in a seventh floor where only six floors were allowed.

Mies van der Rohe, Ludwig (1886–1969) German-American architect, educator, and designer. A perfectionist, his buildings are excellent examples of dynamic space and pure forms created with a refined use of materials. His famous Barcelona chair dates back to the German Pavilion, Barcelona (1929), a classic piece of architecture. His Seagram Building, New York (1958), is another classic in an urban setting.

Nelson, George (b. 1908) American industrial designer, architect, and writer. Following World War II, he intrigued young architects with his books, articles, and industrial design approach to architectural problems.

Neutra, Richard (1892–1970) Austrian-American architect and writer. A pioneer in modern architecture, he is best known for his sophisticated, well-articulated residences with dynamic space flowing out to integrated lanscaping. His early use of structural steel construction and sliding glass doors permitted a transparency as well as an extension of interior spaces.

Palladio, Andrea (1508–1580) Italian architect and writer. Created his own version of Roman architecture. His books, more than his buildings, spread the Palladian influence to England and America some 150 years later.

Rudolph, Paul (b 1918) American architect and educator. His orderly buildings are full of complexity and designed with an imaginative use of materials. Despite a wide range of projects, he is best known for the Art and Architecture Building at Yale University, New Haven (1963), where he was Dean of the School of Architecture.

Saarinen, Eero (1910–1961) Finnish-American architect. A firm believer that each design problem deserves an original and proper solution, his work displays great versatility. His buildings incorporated use of creative building and structural technology. Notable work includes the Dulles Airport, Washington, D.C. (1962); the Jefferson National Expansion Memorial Arch, St. Louis (1968); two residential colleges at Yale University (1962); and the CBS Office Building, New York (1966).

Skidmore, Owings, & Merrill (SOM) (founded 1939) American architectural firm. One of the most successful examples of team practice producing consistent quality architecture. Following their early success in converting corporate clients to modern architecture, they broke through the governmental barrier with their Air Force Academy, Colorado Springs (1955). Their multiple offices developed individual team leaders such as Gordon Bunshaft in New York, Walter Netsch in Chicago, and Charles Bassett in San Francisco.

Stone, Edward D. (b. 1903) American architect. A late bloomer, he did not become well known until 1955 with the plans and model for the American Embassy at New Delhi. Its slender golden columns and the rich texture of the tile grille became identified with his later work although these were not the essence of his designs. His American Pavilion at Brussels (1958) was comparable with other great exhibition structures.

Sullivan, Louis H. (1856–1924) American architect and writer. Leader of the Chicago School of architecture. With his partner, Dankmar Adler, he designed the Auditorium Building, Chicago (1881), the Great Hall of which has recently been restored. The Wainwright Building, St. Louis (1891); the Guaranty Office Building, Buffalo, New York (1895); and the Carson Pirie Scott Store, Chicago (1899) became prototypes of tall, steel-frame structures. He developed exuberant ornamentation in the form of mass-produced panels.

Venturi, Robert (b. 1925) American architect and writer. His work, with partners John Rauch and Denise Scott Brown, delights many young architects with its "outrageous" combination of elements. Recent work includes the Humanities Building, State University of New York at Purchase (1974); and the Bryant House, Greenwich, Connecticut (1976).

Vitruvious Pollio, Marcus (1st century B.C.) Roman architect and writer. He influenced the Renaissance and other Classical revivals through his book *De Architectura*.

Wren, Sir Christopher (1633–1723) British architect, planner, mathematician, and astronomer. While his plan for redesigning the city of London after the Great Fire of 1666 was not adopted, he did participate in the building or rebuilding of some 50 churches in the Classical style. He is best known for his rebuilding of St. Paul's Cathedral.

Wright, Frank Lloyd (1869–1959) American architect, writer, and teacher. A flamboyant and prolific genius, he professed an organic architecture which was expressed in many original forms. A short list of his works includes: Unity Temple, Oak Park, Illinois (1906); Robie House, Chicago (1909); Kaufmann House, or "Falling Water," Bear Run, Pennsylvania (1936); Taliesin West, Phoenix (1934); Johnson Wax Building, Racine, Wisconsin (1936); Beth Shalom Synagogue, Elkins Park, Pennsylvania (1959); and Guggenheim Museum, New York (1959).

Yamasaki, Minoru (b. 1912) American architect. His work shows an emphasis on utility, structure, and delight. Notable work includes the Terminal Building at the St. Louis Airport (firm of Yamasaki, Hellmuth, and Leinweber), 1951; Terminal Building at Dhahran, Saudi Arabia (1963); Science Center at Seattle World's Fair (1965); and World Trade Center, New York (1974).

Question Sets for Evaluating Buildings and How to Use Them

There are many methods of evaluating buildings. Some are very formal. They require a team representing a variety of professionals, numerous interviews, questionnaires, and observations; and they take as many as five years to produce a voluminous report. Others are very casual. They require a minimum of criteria and they involve a maximum of subjectivity. They simply ask the question: "Well, how do you like it?"

The question set method that follows requires that you visit the building in question and make as many observations as may be necessary to answer all 20 questions in the set. If you wish, you may even want to talk to the users and the owners.

Some methods emphasize only one of the major factors which influenced the design of the building. For example, it is common to evaluate a building from the standpoint of its function alone—how a building works to do the job it is supposed to do. Of course, the performance of a building is important, but so is the design quality of its space and form, the response to the client's pocketbook, and the building's time-quality.

What is needed, then, is evaluative criteria which is comprehensive in terms of the major contributing factors: function, form, economy, and time. The criteria should not change appreciably from one building type to another; in other words, the criteria should be fairly consistent. And while the evaluation process must remain subjective, the value measurements should be quantifiable in order to tell at a glance the quality profile of a building.

The modified CRS question sets in this section are intended as comprehensive evaluative criteria. They are not without flaws. However, they are as good as any. And they can be improved.

Read the question, evaluate the building in terms of the question, and give it a number from 1 to 10. The following value measurement scale might be helpful:

Complete failure	1
Critically bad	2
Very poor	3
Poor	4
Acceptable	5
Good	6
Very good	7
Excellent	8
Superior	9
Perfect	10

The final value for each of the four major factors is not necessarily the numerical average of the five individual question responses, but the numerical average can be helpful in determining and understanding each final value.

The graphic profile formed by the final

values shows the relative strengths of each of the four factors.

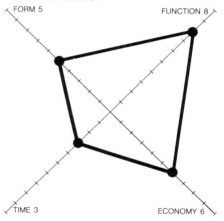

For example, the illustration shows a quadrilateral formed by the following values: function—8, form—5, economy—6, and time—3. We can assume that these values represent the numerical averages of the responses to the five questions in each category.

Remember that each building you evaluate is going to have a different profile. A collection of different graphic profiles can make it easy for you to understand each building's strengths and to make comparisons between buildings.

Don't expect to find a "perfect" building. There isn't one. Perfection is only theoretical. However, good architects feel that the pursuit of perfection is absolutely necessary.

A more sophisticated evaluation would yield a single number, a quality quotient, for each building—one which would represent the equilibrium of the four factors. That sophistication is not appropriate here. However, you may want to refer to *Problem Seeking** for the formula of a quality quotient and for information on which this simplified evaluation technique is based.

Question Sets

The following two question sets cover the same criteria. The difference between them is the format. The full sentence question set is intended for use in the first few evaluations when the meaning and scope of each question is being tested. After a few evaluations, the key word question set, with its abbreviated form and implied wording, may be used to evoke the full meaning of each question quickly.

FULL SENTENCE QUESTION SET

Function

1. How well expressed is **the overall organizational idea,** meaning **the big functional concept?**

2. How **effectively** are the **spaces arranged** and shaped to respond to **functional relationships and goals?**

*W. Peña, W. Caudill, and J. Focke, *Problem Seeking: An Architectural Programming Primer* (Boston: Cahners Books International, 1977).

3. To what degree do the spaces allow **people and/or things to circulate efficiently?**

4. To what extent has **adequate space** been provided—both **programmed** and **unprogrammed** space?

5. To what degree does the building satisfy the **requirements of the user—physical** and **social?**

Form

6. How **imaginatively** conceived is the building as **an expression of originality and excellence?**

7. How well is the **physical environment** enhanced by **controls to provide physical comfort?**

8. How well does the building respond and relate to **the nature of the site** in which it is placed?

9. To what extent are the spaces and forms **enhanced to provide for psychological well being?**

10. How well are the **building systems (structural, mechanical,** and **electrical) integrated or expressed?**

Economy

11. How well does the building embody **appropriate lean simplicity or rich complexity?**

12. To what extent do the materials and their connections respond to **climate and activities** in order to reduce **maintenance and operations costs?**

13. To what extent is the building a **good return for the investment**—"the **most for the money**" idea?

14. To what extent is the building a **realistic solution**, the result of **a balanced budget** through **cost control?**

15. How well do the spaces permit **efficient** operation capitalizing on **elegance,** on **maximum effect with minimum means?**

Time

16. To what extent does the building embody the **spirit** and **expression of the times** in the **use of materials and technology** available at the time?

17. To what extent does the building provide **fixed and tailored spaces for specific activities** likely to **remain static?**

18. To what extent does the building respond to **dynamic changes in function** through **convertible and negotiable spaces?**

19. To what extent does the building **respond to growth** over time—provide for **expansibility?**

20. To what extent do the spaces and forms possess a **sustaining quality**—meaning **vitality and validity over time?**

KEY WORD QUESTION SET

Function

1. **The overall organizational idea** (the big functional concept)

2. **Effective arrangement of spaces** (functional goals and relationships)

3. **Efficient circulation of people and/or things** (flow, movement)

4. **Provision of an adequate amount of space** (programmed, unprogrammed)

5. **Response to user requirements** (physical, social)

Form

6. **Originality and excellence in design** (imagination, quality)

7. **Provisions for physical comfort** (physical environmental controls)

8. **Response to the nature of the site** (site environment)

9. **Provisions for psychological well being** (psychological environment)

10. **Integration or expression of building systems** (structural, mechanical, electrical)

Economy

11. **Appropriate simplicity or complexity** (lean or rich)

12. **Ease of maintenance and operation** (response of materials and connections to climate and activities)

13. **Most for the money** (good return for investment)

14. **Realistic solution to a balanced budget** (cost control)

15. **Maximum effect with minimum means** (elegance, efficiency)

Time

16. **Use of materials and technology of the time** (spirit and expression of the times)

17. **Fixed and tailored spaces for specific activities** (major static activities)

18. **Convertible and negotiable spaces for changes in function** (dynamic activities)

19. **Provision for growth** (expansibility)

20. **Vitality and validity over time** (sustaining quality)

List of Places to Experience Architecture

There are superb buildings, old and new, throughout the United States. Unfortunately, the finest examples are so scattered they are sometimes difficult to reach. Unlike painting, sculpture, and music, buildings must remain on location. You may discover, however, that you have some nationally recognized classics in your own city or a neighboring city.

Identifying outstanding buildings is much easier. For example, the American Institute of Architects, 1735 New York Avenue NW, Washington, D.C. 20006, since 1950 has sponsored the publication of guidebooks which locate architectural landmarks. These are produced regularly every two years to accompany AIA conventions. They are available for most every major city (see pp. 169–170 for a list). If you are specifically interested in old buildings, guides and booklets may be obtained from the Society of Architectural Historians, 1700 Walnut Street, Room 716, Philadelphia, Pennsylvania 19103 (see page 170 for a list). If your search for distinguished buildings is confined to a specific area, contact local architects, the libraries, the tourist bureau, and the Chamber of Commerce. Often museums publish guides. The buildings are there, but it takes some looking.

As you begin to delve into architecture appreciation, becoming more knowledgeable about buildings, increasing your awareness of space and form, raising your level of appreciation, you may find that systematically cataloging certain buildings is a natural means of recording your architectural experiences. You may want to collect photos, slides, and booklets to supplement your own notes as people collect records and tapes of music. In your search for places to experience architecture, you will probably discover unique buildings not in the guides. If so, you may wish to produce your own guide to share with others. Like bird watching, building watching can provide a social function.

Included here is a listing of well-known buildings in certain selected areas. This very limited list is submitted only to help the reader initiate his or her own series of personal tours for experiencing architecture. There is no specific order. Nothing mandatory. No preparation. If some of these buildings are in your area, visit them. If nothing else you'll learn to appreciate space and form by osmosis. A visit to a building is better than reading about it. However, you must be warned: superb buildings are infectious—when you experience them, you'll want to read more about them. And the more you know, the more intense the joy of appreciation. The main thing is to visit good buildings. Hopefully, after reading this book you will have sharpened your visual awareness. If so, familiar buildings will look different to you; so don't mind revisiting them. You don't listen to Beethoven's 5th just once.

The following may help the reader start a series of personal tours of unique, functional, beautiful buildings. "Breaking the ice" is the hardest part. Perhaps visits to just a few of these buildings and building groups will not only be a source of pleasure and learning to you, but will be just what is needed to open up entirely new opportunities for enjoyment.

SAN FRANCISCO AREA

Old Residential Group: A collection of some fine old houses in San Francisco are located in the general area of Pacific Avenue and Presidio Avenue, designed by Willis Polk, Bernard Maybeck, and Ernest Coxhead. Another group is at the end of Vallejo Street on Russian Hill. Polk's own place, now a collection of buildings, is at 1013–1019 Vallejo Street.

First Church of Christ Scientist, Berkeley: This remarkable building, designed by Bernard Maybeck, is located at Bowdich and Dwight Way. One must see the interior.

Greene & Greene Residence, Berkeley: In the same general area is an outstanding old house (now a fraternity house) at 2307 Piedmont designed by the Greene brothers, early pioneers of contemporary design.

University of California, Berkeley: Walking through the campus can be an architectural experience in itself. The Student Center, designed by Vernon De Mars, is worth experiencing. Visit Wurster Hall, designed by De Mars, Don Olsen, and Joseph Esherick, because of the contrast with other buildings. While inside get some architecture professors to recommend other buildings on and off the campus. Hearst Hall, designed by Bernard Maybeck (1899), is one of the better old buildings on the campus, but you must go in to appreciate it.

Bart Stations: The recent rapid transit stations designed by some of the Bay Area's best architects are worth touring. Some are very good.

Hallidie Building: This classic prototype of the glass facade, designed by Willis Polk (1917), is located at 130 Sutter.

Hyatt Regency Hotel: This contemporary structure, designed by John C. Portland and Associates, offers a unique spatial experience in the main lobby.

Oakland Museum, Oakland: A very unusual "site building" that follows the contours, designed by Kevin Roche, John Dinkeloo, and Associates (1969).

Ghirardelli Square: Designed by Wurster, Bernardi, and Emmons, it is located in the Fisherman's Wharf area. This group of rehabilitated space combines the warmth of old structures and the efficiency of new.

The Cannery: This is another successful rehabilitation located in the Fisherman's Wharf area worth experiencing for its many unique spaces and old forms. The architects were Esherick, Homsey, Dodge, and Davis.

University of California, Santa Cruz: The university contains many interesting contemporary buildings designed by San Francisco's best architects.

LOS ANGELES AREA

Gamble House, Pasadena: This house built in 1908 by architects Charles and Henry Greene remains not only one of the finest homes of the famous Greene brothers, but stands out as one of the best examples of excellence for the wood vernacular in America. Conducted tours are available.

Wayfarers' Chapel, Palos Verdes: Built in 1951, the greenhouse-like chapel, designed by Lloyd Wright (son of Frank L. Wright), has been since the day of its dedication, an inspiration to architects and knowledgeable lay people.

Perkins House, Pasadena: A 1955 example of a Richard Neutra–designed house (1540 Poppy Peak Drive). Neutra gave inspiration to many younger men who made variations upon his ideas of space and form. The Los Angeles area has hundreds of quality houses designed by superb architects, but they are hard to find. For more beautiful, functional houses refer to "A Guide to Architecture in Southern California," published by the Los Angeles County Museum of Art. Locations of some excellent Frank Lloyd Wright houses are included in the guide.

University of California at Los Angeles: Experiencing the rich, landscaped vistas has more visual impact than going in and out of individual buildings. Visiting the Sculpture Garden is particularly inspiring. You may want to visit the stadium and the recently constructed Alumni Center.

Pacific Design Center: Designed by Cesar Pelli of Gruen Associates, this all-metal building should be visited not only because of its highly controversial nature, but because of its own spatial order, the fine connections, and contemporary expression. It is located at 8687 Melrose Avenue.

Bradbury Building: This old turn-of-the-century ark is a favorite of architects and particularly of movie-makers, who have used the venerable structure as sets. The outside has nothing to offer whatsoever. But when you go inside, that's a memorable spatial experience. The building is located in the thick of the downtown area across the street from a busy marketplace. George H. Wyman designed the classic cast-iron structure in 1893.

CHICAGO AREA

Auditorium Building (downtown): This is Chicago's most famous cultural building. Located in the central business district (Michigan & Congress), designed by Adler and Sullivan in 1889, and restored by Harry Weese and Associates, unquestionably the Auditorium is an American masterpiece.

Civic Center (downtown): One of the nation's better government buildings, this 31-story steel and glass building was designed by a group of architects and engineers, including C. F. Murphy Associates; Loebl, Schlossman, and Bennett; and Skidmore, Owings, & Merrill. The way the highrise connects the ground to form a civic plaza is worth considerable study.

Illinois Institute of Technology: Created by Mies van der Rohe; Friedman, Alschuler, and Sincere; Holabird and Root; and Pace Associates, the campus is located on South State Street between 31st and 35th. Of special interest are Mies-designed Alumni Memorial Building (1946); the Chapel (1942); and Crown Hall (1956). These buildings exerted tremendous influence on later buildings throughout the United States.

John Hancock Center (downtown): This great giant, designed by Skidmore, Owings, & Merrill, completely dominates its part of the Chicago skyline. Expression of structural logic in silhouette and visual cross bracing is significant.

Robie House: This is one of the most famous houses in the world. Located adjacent to the University of Chicago campus, 5757 South Woodlawn, and designed by Frank Lloyd Wright (1909), the superb residence is considered the finest example of Wright's prairie house. The latest restoration was in 1967. Now it is the Adlai Stevenson Institute of International Affairs.

Reliance Building (downtown): The designer in charge of this project (1894–95) was Charles Atwood of D. H. Burnham and Company. The steel frame, judiciously covered with terra cotta, and the use of large areas of glass make this building a forerunner of many highrises to come. The building is now the 32 North State Building.

Tribune Tower (downtown): This familiar landmark was the result of an international competition (1922). Finished in 1925, the building still remains a controversy although the Gothic revival design won first place. Because of the discussion of the award, architectural historians generally agree that such discussions led to the belief that skyscrapers should not be clad in historical trimmings. Nevertheless, this is a grand old building with its own virtues, particularly the unique silhouettes and interesting treatment of varying-size vertical elements.

COLUMBUS, INDIANA

Touring Columbus, Indiana, is a "must" for every architectural student. The reader might well do the same. This small city is literally a museum of high-quality contemporary buildings—from 1942 to the present. In 1974 the Visitors Center in Columbus published a booklet called "A Look at Architecture," which catalogs these superb buildings and can serve as a guide. There is nothing like Columbus, Indiana, in the world. The great Finnish architect Eliel Saarinen (who most people thought should have won The Chicago Tribune Competition) started it all with the design of the First Christian Church. His even more famous son, Eero Saarinen, followed two decades later by designing the North Christian Church. Some of the best current U.S. architects, including Kevin Roche, John Dinkeloo and Associates; Cesar Pelli of Gruen Associates; Mitchell and Guirgola Associates; I. M. Pei and Partners; Harry Weese; and Gunnar Birkerts have worked in Columbus. It's worth a trip.

HOUSTON AREA

Bishop's Palace, Galveston: This is the best known design by Nicholas J. Clayton—a classic of that era (1888). It's located at 1402 Broadway and open to the public. Sometimes it is referred to as the Walter Gresham House. While in Galveston, visit the Strand (old downtown) to see some most interesting 19th-century stores. And go the University of Texas Medical Branch and visit Old Red, another Clayton masterpiece (1889). While driving on Broadway, you'll see many wonderful buildings.

Astrodome: This is the first of the great sports arenas that brought outside sports inside. It's located on South Loop West and Kirby Drive. Built in 1965, it was designed by Wilson, Morris, Crane, and Anderson, associated with Lloyd, Morgan, and Jones. The tremendous scale can only be sensed from the inside. Inside tours are available.

Tenneco Building (downtown): This is not the latest Houston office building (1963), but it is one of the best. Superbly detailed. Sun controls respect the region. It was designed by Charles Bassett of Skidmore, Owings, & Merrill. The building is located at 1010 Milam.

Pennzoil Place (downtown): Ada Louise Huxtable, *The New York Times* architectural critic, referred to this building as one of the most significant highrises of the decade. Designed in 1976 by Philip Johnson and John Burgee, associated with S. I. Morris Associates, it approaches a pure form of sculpture. If possible, circle the building at a half-mile radius to see the dynamics of the plastic form created by the twin towers. This is more an outside building than an inside building.

Jesse H. Jones Hall for the Performing Arts (downtown): This is a forerunner of a series of multifunction, multiform great halls. It is primarily designed for concerts, opera, ballet, and musicals. The ''house'' can be changed (both physically and acoustically) for 1,800 to 3,000 capacity. The spatially asymmetrical lobby with Richard Leopold's sculpture is worth experiencing. This is more an inside building than an outside building. Charles Lawrence of Caudill Rowlett Scott lead the design effort. The hall (1966) is located at the corner of Texas and Louisiana.

Sam Houston Park (downtown): To experience a collection of early Texas houses (not their original locations), stroll in this park located near the Hyatt Regency. In fact, the contrast of going from the lobby of the hotel to the park with its beautiful, pragmatic Texas houses is a lesson in architectural history. Notice at the edge of the park on the corner there is a two-story building designed by MacKie and Kamrath (1938), the first modern civic building—Houston Fire Alarm Building, now a museum. Houses in the park include Kellum-Noble Residence (1851) and William Marsh Rice Residence (1850), the founder of Rice University.

Rice University: Located at South Main and Sunset, the university is in essence an architectural island on which to spend an enjoyable afternoon experiencing the live oak tree–lined vistas and the interesting buildings. Rice opened for business in 1912 with a good start in carrying out the master plan developed by the famous architect Ralph Adams Cram. Most interesting of all of its buildings is Rice's original Lovett Hall designed in 1910 by Cram, Goodhue, & Ferguson. Some of Houston's best architects have contributed to the many fine modern buildings on the campus, which seem to recognize and respect the fact that Lovett Hall got there first. One of the most elegant structures on the campus is the stadium, designed by Lloyd and Morgan and Milton McGinty in 1950.

Church of the Annunciation: This is a beautiful old stone church (1871) located near downtown. Begun in 1868, it is the oldest church in Houston. The tremendous spire is an amazing engineering feat in any period. Nicholas J. Clayton was the architect. He managed the repairs in 1900. It is located at 1618 Texas Avenue.

Galleria Post Oak: One of the most successful urban places (contains hundreds of shops and fine stores, hotels, clubs, recreational facilities, and theaters) is the Galleria—one of Houston's biggest tourist attractions. It is located on Westheimer and the West Loop. The project was started in 1969, designed by Hellmuth, Obata, Kassabaum with Neuhaus & Taylor, associated architects. Walking around the grand three-level enclosed mall offers an exciting spatial experience. Space and form become alive with the movement of people.

NEW ORLEANS AREA

There has been so much written on New Orleans' buildings, specifically those in the heart of the old French city, that a listing of individual buildings will not be included. However, a walking tour around Jackson Square in the French Quarter—and seeing another world of buildings—can be an enjoyable experience regardless of how many times you have been there. Before you roam, pick up a map or guide and roam with a purpose—to create the best possible climate for making architecture happen.

Not so well known, but equal in architectural importance, is the area called the Garden District, noted for its many fine examples of colonial homes built before the Civil War. You can reach the area by electric streetcar.

ATLANTA AREA

Rhodes Mansion: Pre-Civil War buildings were lost in General Sherman's infamous fire (1865), so Atlanta's visual, architectural history starts thereafter. Since then the city has produced many great buildings, including this castlelike home (1904) designed by W. F. Denny for A. G. Rhodes who, it was said, had seen a castle on the Rhine. It is now used as the Peachtree branch of the State Department of Archives and History.

Robert Griggs Residence, Inman Park: In 1889 Atlanta opened its first electric streetcar line. This led to a new suburb, Inman Park. The intent was to have a picturesque English garden city connected by trolley to large office buildings. The Griggs House (1890), 866 Euclid Avenue, belongs to that important period—the beginning of the bedroom community. By 1960 Inman Park had become a slum area, but today there has been much restoration—as was the case of this house restored in 1969.

Georgia State Capitol (downtown): Located on Washington and Mitchell streets and dominating the immediate neighborhood skyline with its accented gold dome, the Capitol commands the respect generally associated with buildings of a similar nature. The Chicago firm of Edbooke and Burnham designed the structure in 1889.

Hyatt-Regency Hotel (downtown): If you have seen the Hyatt-Regency hotels in Houston, Chicago, and San Francisco, see this one too. Here is the grandparent of them all. The trademark—the skyhigh lobby—was first used here. The hotel was designed by Edwards and Portman in 1966 and is located at 265 Peachtree Street NE.

Equitable Building (downtown): Every major city seems to have a Skidmore, Owings, & Merrill office building. Here is Atlanta's. Built in 1968, the project was done in association with Finch, Alexander, Barnes, Rothschild, and Paschal. The address is 100 Peachtree Street.

Omni (near downtown): If you wish to experience the massive scale of an indoor sports arena, visit this giant structure, 100 Techwood Drive Viaduct NW. Built in 1972, the architects were Thompson, Ventulett, & Stainback.

Wren's Nest: This is an early Atlanta shingle-style cottage. A main feature is the large veranda still in its original condition. The cottage belonged to Joel Chandler Harris who completed it in 1885. The address is 1050 Gordon Street SW.

Martin Luther King, Jr., Birthplace: Another example of houses built just before the turn of the century is the birthplace of Dr. King at 500 Auburn Avenue NE. It's a well-preserved and restored city house (on a small lot, but two-storied) representative of that period.

SAVANNAH, GEORGIA

Walking the sidewalks and through the squares of Savannah is pure joy to the knowledgeable person. If you know little about buildings, you'll be considerably more informed after such a walking tour. Savannah is a lovely, beautiful, old city. It's not a case of having history, it is history. James Oglethorpe started it all in 1733. The old section has the architectural simplicity he meant it to have—common squares that neighbors share. It wasn't designed for automobiles, but for walking; so walk. Guidebooks are available. You'll experience the oasislike squares of the first settlement, the 18th-century cottages, mansions of the 19th-century merchants, and the wharves and warehouses of that period when Savannah was the world's trading center for cotton. Although you will thoroughly enjoy seeing the wonderful old buildings, it is the spaces between them, you'll find, that will raise your level of architecture appreciation.

NEW YORK CITY

Seagram Building (midtown): This is the building that architects consider the ultimate summation of refinement for steel and glass skyscrapers. The connections are superb. Mies van der Rohe led the design effort with Philip Johnson and Kahn & Jacobs (1958). You'll find the building at 375 Park Avenue between 52nd and 53rd Streets. Note the interesting contrast (pleasing to most people) between this 20th-century building and nearby 19th-century masonry structures.

Grand Central Terminal (midtown): Experience the great lobby. Find a place on the landing of the upper stairs at rush hour to witness the moving current of people below. It's quite a sight—"the container equals the contained." The old terminal at 42nd Street and Park Avenue was built in 1913 and designed by Reed & Stem and Warren & Wetmore.

St. Patrick's Cathedral (midtown): This is not the oldest nor the biggest church in the city, but it has the most unique setting—in the thick of things on Fifth Avenue across from Rockefeller Plaza. The architect, James Renwick, created an adaptation (1858–1879) of French Gothic. The 330-foot twin towers do quite well competing with the surrounding skyscrapers.

Lever House (midtown): This one arrived on the Manhattan scene before the Seagram Building. It remains an architectural landmark. The owners gave part of their land back to the people by using only a fraction of the allowable building volume permitted by zoning laws. It was the first (1952) of the "prestige" glass-walled buildings. You'll find it at 390 Park Avenue between 53rd and 54th Streets. It was designed by Skidmore, Owings, & Merrill.

Cathedral of St. John the Divine (Central Park area): It's located just north of Central Park on Amsterdam Avenue at 112th Street. This is the largest church of modern times. It has a magnificent interior, the scale of which is very hard to describe. You have to experience it. Begun in 1892, three different architectural firms have worked on it—Heins & LaFarge; Cram & Ferguson; Adams & Woodbridge. Ralph Adam Cram redesigned the cathedral within the French Gothic vernacular. Although in use, the great building is still unfinished, but most cathedrals never were.

Solomon R. Guggenheim Musem (Central Park area): This world famous building by Frank Lloyd Wright (1959) is located on Fifth Avenue between 88th and 89th Streets across from Central Park. It's a classic in curvilinear plastic form. Experiencing the central space will stay with you.

Brooklyn Bridge (lower Manhattan): If you are looking for historical monuments, experience this old structure—a highly functional, super urban ornament having a strong time quality but also a wonderful sustaining quality. This great "building" without walls or roof spans the East River between Brooklyn and lower Manhattan near City Hall Park. If you are really ambitious, walk the Bridge—a unique kinetic experience. While you are there, view Manhattan from Brooklyn Heights—an unforgettable sight.

Brooklyn Bridge opened for riding and walking in 1883. It took 14 years to build—in the same period the telephone and electric light were introduced. If you want to prepare yourself by delving deep into its history, read *The Great Bridge* by David McCullough, an interesting book on building this great monument. In any case, treat yourself to a different kind of architectural experience.

Ford Foundation Building (midtown): This is far from being just another office building. The lobby is parklike. It's good fun just to walk through. You find it on East 42nd Street between First and Second Avenues. Kevin Roche and John Dinkeloo were the architects (1967).

BOSTON AREA

Trinity Church (Back Bay): This is Henry Hobson Richardson's best work, according to most architectural historians. He won his commission in a competition (1872). It's a magnificent church in the masculine Romanesque in which Richardson excelled. While you are at Copley Square (1883), enjoy the contrasting John Hancock Tower (1973) by I. M. Pei and Partners (you can't miss it); Boston Public Library (1887) by McKim, Mead, & White; and New Old South Church (1874) by Cummings & Sears. If you visit Boston, you must spend time around Copley Square.

Boston University (Charles River area): The Schools of Law and Education Building (1964) had a great impact on young architects at the time it was designed. The concrete structure was in tune with the time when "the heavies" were popular. It was designed by Sert, Jackson, & Gourley with Edwin T. Steffian.

Harvard University, Cambridge: It's a big place, but it's full of interesting buildings, old and new. You should experience Harvard Yard, of course. That's Old Harvard. Contemporary Harvard is seeing the first Harvard Graduate Center (1949) by The Architects Collaborative, then under the strong leadership of the great teacher/architect Walter Gropius. It's located at 14 Everett Street. You should visit the rare Carpenter Center for the Visual Arts (1963), 19 Prescott Street, designed by LeCorbusier with Sert, Jackson, & Gourley; and Peabody Terrace (1963), 900 Memorial Drive by Sert, Jackson, & Gourley.

Massachusetts Institute of Technology, Cambridge: A visit to four outstanding buildings will make an afternoon or morning well spent. The first is a design by world-famous architect Alvar Aalto with Perry, Shaw, & Hepburn. It's the Baker House (1947–1949), 362 Memorial Drive. Close by is the MIT Chapel (1955) designed by Eero Saarinen. And adjacent to the chapel is the Student Union (1963), 84 Massachusetts Avenue, by Eduardo Catalano with Brannen & Shimamoto. The fourth is across Massachusetts Avenue on the main campus. It's the Green Building (1964) designed by I. M. Pei and Partners.

New City Hall (downtown): This bold, impressive structure (1968) with its maze of interlocking spaces and forms is the focal point of the new Government Center planned by I. M. Pei. The design of the City Hall itself came as the result of a national competition. There were 250 entries from which eight finalists were chosen. The winner turned out to be a team of young, relatively unknown, architects—Kallmann, McKinnen, & Knowles who are associated with Campbell, Aldrich, & Nulty, and with LeMessurier and Associates. There was much publicity given to the design, with criticisms ranging from its being a tour-de-force to its being a creative, functional solution making use of highly artistic composition of intricate spaces and forms conveying the spirit of the times. Boston was ready for it. It's been good for Boston.

State House (Beacon Hill): This grand old building (1798), located on Beacon and Park streets, was designed by Charles Bulfinch. The rear extension (1895) was by Charles E. Brigham. And the wings were added in 1916 by R. Clipston Sturgis. Try to visit this old one the same day you visit the new City Hall. You'll learn a history lesson.

Beacon Hill Dwelling (Beacon Hill): Walk the area between Beacon and Cambridge streets and from Bowdoin Street to the Charles River. It will take you out of this world and put you in the 19th century. There's a human quality there you'll always remember. Pick up a guide book (they are plentiful in Boston) and locate a few of the outstanding buildings and building groups such as Louisburg Square (1837); Sears House (now the Somerset Club) designed by Alexander Parris in 1818; the apartments at 13-17 Chestnut Street (1818) by Charles Bulfinch; and Women's City Club (1805), also by Bulfinch.

Old Town, Salem: The immediate area outside of Boston is rich with historical buildings and early civic spaces. The old town at Salem is particularly worthwhile. Plan a driving tour which includes Concord and Lexington, west of Boston; Cohasset, Hingham, and Plymouth, south of Boston; and Marblehead, Salem, and Gloucester, north of Boston. That's where it all started.

The reason for including "List of Places to Experience Architecture" in this book is more to whet the reader's appetite than to lay out specific tours. So plan your own tour. There's fun in planning. Since the prime purpose of the book is to help you increase your appreciation for space and form, consider planning and conducting your own tour. (If you do one, you'll do others.) There are no better exercises to hone architecture appreciation.

AIA LIBRARY BIBLIOGRAPHY '77: CONVENTION CITY GUIDEBOOKS

1952: Jackson, Huson. *New York Architecture, 1650–1952.* New York: Reinhold, 1952. NA735. N5J3.

1953: Steinbrueck, Victor. *Seattle Architecture, 1850–1953.* New York: Reinhold, 1953. NA735 .S45S8.

1954: Hitchcock, Henry Russell. *Boston Architecture, 1637–1954; Including Other Communities within Easy Driving Distance.* New York: Reinhold, 1954. NA735 .B6H5.

1955: McClure, Harlan Ewart. *Twin Cities Architecture; Minneapolis and St. Paul, 1820–1955.* New York: Reinhold, 1955. NA735 .M5M3.

1956: Honnold, Douglas. *Southern California Architecture, 1769–1956.* New York: Reinhold, 1956. NA730 .C2H6.

1957: American Institute of Architects, Washington Metropolitan Chapter. *Washington Architecture, 1791–1957.* NA735 .W3A6.

1958: American Institute of Architects, Cleveland Chapter. *Cleveland Architecture, 1796–1958.* New York: Reinhold, 1958. NA735 .C6A7.

1959: Samuel Wilson, Jr., American Institute of Architects, New Orleans Chapter. *A Guide to the Architecture of New Orleans, 1699–1959.* New York: Reinhold, 1959. NA735 .N4A7.

1960: Woodbridge, John Marshall, and Sally Byrne Woodbridge. *Buildings of the Bay Area: A Guide to the Architecture of the San Francisco Bay Region.* New York: Grove Press, 1960. NA735 .S35W6.

1961: American Institute of Architects, Philadelphia Chapter. *Philadelphia Architecture.* New York: Reinhold, 1961. NA735 .P5A7.

1962: American Institute of Architects, Dallas Chapter. *The Prairie's Yield: Forces Shaping Dallas Architecture from 1840 to 1962.* New York: Reinhold, 1962. NA735 .D2A4.

1963: American Institute of Architects, Florida South Chapter. *A Guide to the Architecture of Miami.* Miami, 1963. NA735 .M4A5.

1964: McCue, George, American Institute of Architects, St. Louis Chapter. *The Building Art in St. Louis: Two Centuries; A Guide to the Architecture of the City and Its Environs.* St. Louis: St. Louis Chapter, American Institute of Architects, 1964. NA735 .S2M3. Rev. ed., 1967. NA735 .S2M3 1967.

1965: American Institute of Architects, Washington Metropolitan Chapter. *A Guide to the Architecture of Washington, D.C.* Washington, D.C., 1965. NA735 .W3A62.

1966: Jackson, Olga. *Architecture / Colorado.* Denver: Colorado Chapter, American Institute of Architects, 1966. NA730 .C6J3.

1967: Norval White and Elliot Willensky, eds., American Institute of Architects, New York Chapter. *AIA Guide to New York City.* New York, 1967. NA735 .N5A5. Later edition with index. New York: Macmillan, 1968. NA735 .N5A5 1968.

1968: American Institute of Architects, Portland, Oregon, Chapter. *A Guide to Portland Architecture.* Portland, Ore., 1968. NA735 .P55A5.

1969: Siegel, Arthur S., *Chicago's Famous Buildings: A Photographic Guide to the City's Architectural Landmarks and Other Notable Buildings.* 2d ed., rev. and enlarged. Chicago: University of Chicago Press, 1969. NA735 .C4S52 1969.

1970: Donald Freeman, ed., Boston Society of Architects. *Boston Architecture.* Cambridge, Mass.: MIT Press, 1970. NA735 .B6B6.

1971: Katharine M. Meyer, ed. *Detroit Architecture: AIA Guide.* Detroit: Wayne State University Press, 1971. NA735 .D4D4.

1972: *Houston: An Architectural Guide.* Houston: Houston Chapter, American Institute of Architects, 1972. NA735 .H68H6.

1973: David Gebhard et al.: *A Guide to Architecture in San Francisco and Northern California.* Santa Barbara: Peregrine Smith, 1973. NA735 .S35G83.

1974: American Institute of Architects, Washington Metropolitan Chapter. *A Guide to the Architecture of Washington, D.C.* 2d ed., rev. and expanded. New York: McGraw-Hill, 1974. NA735 .W3A62 1974.

1975: American Institute of Architects, Atlanta Chapter. *The American Institute of Architects Guide to Atlanta.* Atlanta, 1975. NA735 .A9A4.

1976: American Institute of Architects, Philadelphia Chapter. *Phila. Pa.: AIA's Abbreviated Guide; Everything You'd Like to Know, But No More.* Philadelphia, 1976. NA735 .P5A6.

Guides and Booklets Available from the Society of Architectural Historians

Listed alphabetically by state and alphabetically by title within state.

A Guide to Architecture in San Francisco and Northern California, by David Gebhard, Roger Montgomery, Robert Winter, John Woodbridge, and Sally Woodbridge.

A Greene and Greene Guide, by Janann Strand.

A Guide to the Work of Greene and Greene, by Randell L. Makinson.

Architectural Guide to San Diego, San Diego. Chapter, AIA.

L.A. in the Thirties—1931–1941, by David Gebhard and Harriette Von Breton.

Photographic Guide to the University of California, Berkeley, by Benjamin B. Ehrich.

Santa Cruz Historic Building Survey, prepared for the City of Santa Cruz by Charles Hall Page & Associates, Inc.

New Haven: A Guide to Architecture and Urban Design, by Elizabeth Mills Brown.

Norwich, Connecticut: A Guide to Its Architecture, by Stephen W. Harby.

A Guide to the Architecture of Washington, D.C., Washington Metropolitan Chapter, AIA (written and edited by Warren J. Cox, Hugh Newell Jacobsen, Francis D. Lethbridge, and David R. Rosenthal).

Walking Tours: Washington, D.C., by Tony P. Wrenn.

The Houses of St. Augustine 1565–1821, by Albert Manucy.

Old Honolulu: A Guide to Oahu's Historic Buildings, Historic Buildings Task Force.

Saints & Oddfellows: A Bicentennial Sampler of Idaho Architecture, by J. Meredith Neil.

Chicago's Famous Buildings, Arthur Siegel, ed.

Chicago's Landmark Structures: An Inventory, vol. 1 and 2, Landmarks Preservation Council and Service.

Faith & Form: Synagogue Architecture in Illinois, by Arthur M. Feldman, Grace C. Grossman, Lauren W. Rader, and Morris A. Gutstein.

Guide to Frank Lloyd Wright and Prairie School Architecture in Oak Park, by Paul E Sprague.

A Guide to New Orleans Architecture, New Orleans Chapter, AIA.

Historic Architecture of Maine (HABS catalog), by Denys Peter Myers.

Amherst: A Guide to Its Architecture, by Paul F. Norton.

The Cape Cod House: An Introductory Study, by Ernest Allen Connally.

Guide to Cambridge Architecture: Ten Walking Tours, by Robert B. Rettig.

This Other Gloucester: Occasional Papers on the Arts of Cape Ann, Massachusetts, by James F. O'Gorman.

Victorian Boston Today: Ten Walking Tours, New England Chapter, Victorian Society in America, Pauline Chase Harrell and Margaret Supplee Smith, eds.

Detroit Architecture: AIA Guide, Katharine Mattingly Meyer, ed.

New Jersey's Historic Houses, by Sibyl McC. Groff.

New Mexico Architecture (Guide to Historic Architecture in Northern New Mexico), by Bainbridge Bunting and John Conron.

Architecture in Westfield (N.Y.), by Marlene and Therold Lindquist.

Cast-Iron Architecture in New York, by Margot Gayle and Edmund V. Gillon, Jr.

Landmarks of Dutchess County, 1683–1867, Dutchess County Planning Board.

Landmarks of Rochester and Monroe County, by Paul Malo.

Mansions, Mills, and Main Streets: Buildings and Places to Explore Within 50 Miles of New York City, by Carole Rifkind and Carol Levine.

The Nineteenth-Century Architecture of Saratoga Springs, by Stephen S. Prokopoff and Joan C. Siegfried.

Wood and Stone: Landmarks of the Upper Mohawk Region, by Virginia B. Kelly, Merrilyn R. O'Connell, Stephen S. Olney, and Johanna R. Reig.

Our Valley . . . Our Villages: An Illustrated Story of the Chagrin Valley (Ohio), by Richard N. Campen.

Bicentennial City: Walking Tours of Historic Philadelphia, by John Francis Marion.

Building Early America (Proceedings of Symposium Held at Philadelphia in 1974 by the Carpenters' Company), Charles E. Peterson, ed.

Fairmount Park: A History and a Guidebook, by Esther M. Klein.

Philadelphia Georgian: The City House of Samuel Powel and Some of its Eighteenth-Century Neighbors, by George B. Tatum.

Newport: A Tour Guide, rev. ed., by Anne L. Randall and Robert P. Foley.

Rhode Island: An Historical Guide, by Sheila Steinberg and Cathleen McGuigan.

Nashville: A Short Historic and Selected Buildings, Eleanor Graham, ed.

Texas Catalog: Historic American Buildings Survey, compiled by Paul Goeldner; Lucy Pope Wheeler and S. Allen Chambers, Jr., eds.

Exploring Vancouver (Official Guidebook, Greater Vancouver Chapter, Architectural Institute of British Columbia), by Harold Kalman.

Europe Architectural Guide 1860–Today, by Jerryll Habegger.

Selected Reading List

American Architecture and Urbanism by Vincent Scully. New York: Praeger, 1969. This book is concerned with the meaning of American building. Vincent Scully, one of America's most brilliant architectural historians, defines architecture as "a continuing dialogue between generations which creates an environment across time." In this book, Scully points out that building design and city planning are not only two related subjects, but are inseparable in both immediate effect and ultimate significance because "every citizen must now share an active and critical responsibility for the failure of the American city." An important book, profusely illustrated.

American Building, The Historical Forces that Shaped It by James Marston Fitch. 2d ed., rev. and enlarged. Boston: Houghton Mifflin, 1948. Although this book was originally published 30 years ago, Professor James Marston Fitch of Columbia University wrote it to be read today. He says, "American building today shows immense potentials; it also has great deficiencies. To be able to discriminate between the two is thus a question of first-rate importance to everyone. For here, as elsewhere, an informed public is the prerequisite to closing the gap between what we *could* do and what we *are* doing." Through a brief history, Fitch traces the main forces which have shaped American building and then synthesizes those aspects of contemporary architectural theory and practice which he feels are important. This fascinating book is well illustrated.

Architecture: A Book of Projects for Young Adults by Forrest Wilson. New York: Reinhold Book Corp., 1968. This beautifully illustrated primer introduces the reader to the architectural alphabet (the principles of building) and then to the words of the architectural language (such as texture, scale, and space). If you like this little primer, there are four others by the same author.

The Architecture Book by Norval White, New York: Alfred A. Knopf, 1976. A splendid compendium of architects and their famous projects, architectural history, terminology, and techniques. This book is written for the layperson and it is fully illustrated. Professionals will find this a witty dictionary.

The Architecture of Humanism by Geoffrey Scott. Gloucester, Mass.: Peter Smith, 1965. This book was first published in 1914. It delves into the essence of what architecture is all about—people. It's an excellent study of the relationship of the history of taste to the history of ideas. Chapter 8 (on humanist values), which discusses line, space, voids/solids, mass, scale, and order, is particularly interesting and appropriate for today.

Complexity and Contradiction in Architecture by Robert Venturi. The Museum of Modern Art Papers on Architecture #1. New York: The Museum of Modern Art, 1966 (paperback). Robert Venturi's book opposes what many would consider the Establishment or, at least, established opinion. According to Professor Vincent Scully of Yale, this is probably the most important writing on building design since Le Corbusier's *Vers une Architecture (Towards a New Architecture)*, published in 1923. Where Le Corbusier demanded a noble purism in architecture, in single buildings and cities as a whole, Venturi welcomes the contradictions and complexities of urban experience at all scales. "As an artist," he says, "I frankly write about what I like in architecture: complexity and contradiction." By doing so, he aims for vitality as well as validity. You may not like what you read, but it's required reading for serious students of serious buildings. A difficult, provocative book, but well worth the effort.

Experiencing Architecture by Steen Eiler Rasmussen. Copenhagen: Krohns Bogtrykkeri, 1957; London: Chapman and Hall, 1959 (available in paperback); and Cambridge, Mass.: MIT Press, 1962. A classic on the subject of experiencing architecture. A simply titled and simply written book on the fundamentals of architectural space, scale, proportion, rhythm, texture, daylighting, color, sound, and more. By far, the best book on appreciation. Excellent reading.

Form and Function: Remarks on Art, Design, and Architecture by Horatio Greenough. Berkeley and Los Angeles: University of California Press, 1947 (paperback). Horatio Greenough (1805–1852), a less than great American sculptor and painter, nevertheless had concepts related to buildings which were generations ahead of his time. He reads today like a progressive contemporary. Louis Sullivan unquestionably was influenced by his writings. And, of course, Sullivan was Frank Lloyd Wright's mentor. It was Greenough, not Whitman, who first protested against meaningless ornamentation. It was Greenough, not Ruskin, who first expressed the idea that the buildings and art of a people express their morality. It was Greenough, not Le Corbusier, who first said that buildings designed primarily for use "may be called machines." It's good to get to the original source. The chapter on American architecture is most appropriate.

Great Architecture of the World, edited by John Julius Norwich. New York: Random House, and London: Mitchell Beazley Publishers Ltd., 1975. A magnificently illustrated book that traces humanity's finest architectural achievements from prehistory to present day. The book tells how to distinguish one style from another and explains the social and cultural forces that led to the creation of each style. Beautiful cutaway drawings reveal details of design and construction which a camera could never capture; the reader can see *how* a building works. There are nearly 800 illustrations, over 440 in full color. A great reference book.

The Master Builders by Peter Blake. New York: Alfred A. Knopf, 1960. Here is a book about three great modern architects: Le Corbusier, Mies van der Rohe, and Frank Lloyd Wright—their lives, their philosophies, and their work. Written by Peter Blake, a superb historian, the book makes these three influential architects/artists come alive, providing interesting facts behind their famous projects. This is not a picture book, but it is well illustrated with drawings and photographs.

A Pictorial History of Architecture in America by G. E. Kidder Smith. 2 vols. New York: American Heritage Publishing Co., 1976. The author is an expert in architectural photography. Arranged by geographical area, this is a superb visual documentation of not only the "great structures from most periods of the nation's history and many little-known, but rewarding, examples of regional and vernacular architecture."

Towards a New Architecture by Le Corbusier. London: The Architectural Press, 1927. This little book was originally published in Paris in 1923 and has had a tremendous influence on architects throughout the world. The English translation (1927) gave this country the first explanation of the "Modern Movement." For a period of time, Harvard University's School of Design used it as a bible. So did the thousands of "Corbu's followers" in the profession of architecture. His writings have the same simple clarity as his buildings.

Credits

Photographs are identified by page number.

Frontispiece: Richards Medical Research Building, University of Pennsylvania. Architect: Louis Kahn. Photographer: John Ebstel.

7: Thomas Hall for the Performing Arts, University of Akron. Architect: CRS Inc./Dalton, Van Dijk, Johnson, & Partners. Photographer: Bruce Kiefer.

8: Thomas Hall for the Performing Arts, University of Akron. Architects: CRS Inc./Dalton, Van Dijk, Johnson, & Partners. Photographer: Balthazar Korab.

11, top left: Residence, Houston, Texas. Architect: Charles Lawrence. Photographer: Rick Gardner.

11, top right: Fodrea Elementary School, Columbus, Ohio. Architect: CRS Inc./A. Dean Taylor. Photographer: Balthazar Korab.

11, bottom left: Kimbell Art Museum, Fort Worth, Texas. Architect: Louis Kahn. Photographer: Ezra Stoller.

11, bottom right: Charles Schorre Studio, Houston, Texas. Photographer: Rick Gardner.

13: Roofscape, Rome. Photographer: Balthazar Korab.

14, top left: St. Lukes and Texas Children's Hospital, Houston, Texas. Architect: CRS Inc. Photographer: Rob Muir.

14, top right: CRS Office, Houston, Texas. Architect: CRS Inc. Photographer: Jim Parker.

14, bottom right: Courthouse Center, Columbus, Indiana. Architect: Cesar Pelli of Gruen Associates. Photographer: Balthazar Korab.

17, top: Rotunda, Texas State Capitol, Austin, Texas. Architect: E. E. Myers. Photographer: Rick Gardner.

17, bottom: Guggenheim Museum, New York, New York. Architect: Frank Lloyd Wright. Photographer: Julius Shulman.

19, top: Greeley National Bank, Greeley, Colorado. Architect: Neil Carpenter. Photographer: Rick Gardner.

19, bottom: Residence, Santa Barbara, California. Architect: Richard J. Neutra. Photographer: Julius Shulman.

20, top left: Residence, Houston, Texas. Architect: W. T. Cannady. Photographer: Rick Gardner.

20, top right: Kahala Hilton Hotel, Honolulu, Hawaii. Architect: Killingsworth, Brady, & Associates. Photographer: Julius Shulman.

20, bottom left: Kentucky State Capitol, Frankfort, Kentucky. Photographer: Balthazar Korab.

20, bottom right: Residence, Houston, Texas. Architect: Howard Barnstone. Photographer: Rick Gardner.

21, top: Calder Plaza, Grand Rapids, Michigan. Photograph: Courtesy Herman Miller Inc.

21, bottom: Hyatt Regency, O'Hare Airport, Chicago, Illinois. Architect: John Portman. Photographer: Balthazar Korab.

22: Roy E. Larsen Hall, Harvard University, Cambridge, Mass. Architect: CRS Inc.

23: Hagia Sophia, Istanbul, Turkey. Photograph: Courtesy Bettmann Archive.

24, top left: Lake Point Tower, Chicago, Illinois. Architect: Schippeit & Heinrich. Photographer: Hedrich Blessing.

24, top right: Styles/Morse Colleges, Yale University, New Haven, Connecticut. Architect: Eero Saarinen. Photographer: Balthazar Korab.

24, bottom left: Furniture by Herman Miller Inc., Zeeland, Michigan. Photograph: Courtesy Herman Miller Inc.

24, bottom right: Photographer: Balthazar Korab.

26: Crown Hall, Illinois Institute of Technology, Chicago, Illinois. Architect: Ludwig Mies van der Rohe. Photographer: Balthazar Korab.

27: Cathedral of Notre Dame, Paris. Architecture begun by Bishop Maurice de Sully in 1163. Photograph: Courtesy Bettmann Archive.

28, top left: Submarine Training Base, U.S. Navy, San Diego, Calif. Architect: Ward Deems. Photographer: Julius Shulman.

28, top right: Residence (built 1874), Schulenberg, Texas. Photographer: Rick Gardner.

28, bottom left: Commonwealth Bank, Toronto, Canada. Architect: Ludwig Mies van der Rohe. Photographer: Balthazar Korab.

28, bottom right: Hagadone Newspapers Corporate Headquarters, Coeur d'Alene, Idaho. Architect: Richard Nelson. Photographer: Julius Shulman.

30: German Pavilion, International Exposition 1929, Barcelona. Architect: Ludwig Mies van der Rohe. Photograph: Courtesy The Museum of Modern Art, New York.

31: Christian Science Organization Building, University of Illinois, Urbana, Illinois. Architect: Paul Rudolph. Photographer: Hedrich Blessing.

32, top left: University Reformed Church, Ann Arbor, Michigan. Architect: Gunnar-Birkerts & Associates. Photographer: Balthazar Korab.

32, top right: Residence, Pasadena, California. Architect: Thornton Ladd. Photographer: Julius Shulman.

32, bottom left: Fountain, Portland, Oregon. Landscape Architect: Larry Halprin. Photographer: Julius Shulman.

32, bottom right: Carpenter Center for the Visual Arts, Harvard University, Cambridge, Massachusetts. Architect: LeCorbusier. Photographer: Balthazar Korab.

33: Dulles International Airport, Washington, D.C. Architect: Eero Saarinen. Photographer: Balthazar Korab.

34: Charles Schorre Studio, Houston, Texas. Photographer: Rick Gardner.

35, top left: Capital National Bank, Houston, Texas. Architect: CRS Inc. Photographer: John Bintliff.

35, top right: National Galerie: Museum of 20th Century Art, Berlin. Architect: Ludwig Mies van der Rohe. Photographer: Balthazar Korab.

35, bottom: CRS Office, Houston, Texas. Architect: CRS Inc. Photographer: Ron Partridge.

36, top left: Irwin Union Bank & Trust Company, Columbus, Indiana. Architect: CRS Inc.

36, top right: Residence, Los Angeles, California. Architect: Irving Gill. Photographer: Julius Shulman.

36, bottom: Black Elementary School, Mesquite, Texas. Architect: CRS Inc. Photographer: Ulric-Meisel.

37, top left: Worcester Art Museum, Worcester, Mass. Architect: The Architects Collaborative. Photograph: Ezra Stoller.

37, top right: Opelika High School, Opelika, Ala. Architect: CRS Inc./Lancaster & Lancaster. Photographer: James Brett.

37, bottom left: Cranbrook Institute, Bloomfield Hills, Michigan. Architect: Eliel Saarinen. Photographer: Balthazar Korab.

37, bottom right: Westinghouse Nuclear Research Center, Monroeville, Pennsylvania. Architect: Deeter, Ritchey, Sippel Associates. Photographer: Balthazar Korab.

38: Roofscape, Rome. Photographer: Balthazar Korab.

39, top: San Jacinto Elementary School, Liberty Texas. Architect: CRS Inc. Photographer: Ulric-Meisel.

39, bottom: George Fulton Mansion (built 1872–1875), Fulton Beach, Texas. Photographer: Rick Gardner.

40: Calder Plaza, Grand Rapids, Mich. Photograph: Courtesy Herman Miller Inc.

41, top: Christian Science Church, Berkeley, California. Architect: Bernard Maybeck. Photographer: Julius Shulman.

41, bottom: Mt. Vernon Dormitory, Washington, D.C. Architect: Hartman-Cox. Photograph: Courtesy Hartman-Cox Architects.

42, top: Residence, Houston, Texas. Architect: William Caudill. Photographer: Jim Parker.

42, bottom: G.M. Technical Center, Styling Section, Domed Auditorium, Detroit, Michigan. Architect: Eero Saarinen. Photographer: Balthazar Korab.

43: Lawrence Residence, Houston, Texas. Architect: Charles Lawrence. Photographer: Julius Shulman.

44: TWA Terminal, New York. Architect: Eero Saarinen. Photographer: Balthazar Korab.

45: Residence, Santa Barbara, California. Architect: Richard J. Neutra. Photographer: Julius Shulman.

46, top: Fodrea Elementary School, Columbus, Ind. Architect: CRS Inc./A. Dean Taylor. Photographer: Balthazar Korab.

46, bottom: Residence (built 1908), Pasadena, California. Architect: Greene & Greene. Photograph: Julius Shulman.

47: Residence, Houston, Texas. Architect: Charles Lawrence. Photographer: Julius Shulman.

48, top: Residence, Houston, Texas. Architect: Howard Barnstone. Photographer: Rick Gardner.

48, middle: Blackwell Senior High School, Blackwell, Oklahoma. Architect: CRS Inc./Philip A. Wilber. Photographer: Bob Hawks, Inc.

101, bottom left: Elementary School, Blackwell, Oklahoma. Architect: CRS Inc./Philip A. Wilber. Photographer: Julius Shulman.

101, bottom right: Wilson Elementary School, Miami, Oklahoma. Architect: CRS Inc. Photographer: Ulric Meisel.

102: Physio Control Corp., Redmond, Washington. Architect: Kirk, Wallace, McKinley, & Associates. Photograph: Courtesy Kirk, Wallace, McKinley, & Associates.

103: Guggenheim Museum, New York, New York. Architect: Frank Lloyd Wright. Photographer: Julius Shulman.

104: Jones Hall for the Performing Arts, Houston, Texas. Architect: CRS Inc.

105, top: CRS Office, Houston, Texas. Architect: CRS Inc. Photographer: Ron Partridge.

105, bottom: Desert Samaritan Hospital, Mesa, Arizona. Architect: CRS Inc./Drover, Welch, & Lindlan Architects. Photographer: Jim Parker.

106: Pima County Junior College, Tucson, Arizona. Architect: CRS Inc./William Wilde/Friedman & Jobusch. Photographer: Julius Shulman.

108: Dedication of the Zuni Comprehensive Health Center, Zuni, New Mexico. Architect: CRS Inc./Chambers, Campbell, Isaacson, & Chaplin, Inc. Photographer: Doyle Wayman.

109: Photographer: Balthazar Korab.

110: Charlottesville High School, Charlottesville, Virginia. Architect: CRS Inc./Stainback & Scribner Associates. Photographer: Jim Parker.

111: Mission Viejo Elementary School, Aurora, Colorado. Architect: CRS Inc./William C. Haldeman. Photographer: Jim Parker.

112: Texas State Capitol (built 1882–1888), Austin, Texas. Architect: E. E. Myers. Photographer: Balthazar Korab.

113: Marina City, Chicago, Illinois. Architect: Bertram Goldberg. Photographer: Heidrich Blessing.

114: University of Petroleum & Minerals, Saudi Arabia. Architect: CRS Inc.

115: North Christian Church, Columbus, Indiana. Architect: Eero Saarinen. Photographer: Balthazar Korab.

116: Mummers Theater, Oklahoma City, Oklahoma. Architect: John M. Johansen. Photographer: Balthazar Korab.

119: Cypress College, Fullerton, California. Architect: CRS Inc./William E. Blurock & Partners/Taylor & Conner. Photographer: Julius Shulman.

120, top: Sauk Valley College, Sterling, Illinois. Architect: CRS Inc./Durrant, Deininger, Dommer, Kramer, Gordon. Photographer: Bill Hedrich.

120, bottom: William Rainey Harper College, Palatine, Illinois. Architect: CRS Inc. Photographer: Ron Partridge.

121, top and bottom: San Francisco Bay Area Rapid Transit District Station, San Francisco, California. Arthitect: Esherick, Homsey, Dodge, & Davis. Photographer: Wayne Thom.

122, top: Underwood Elementary School, Andrews, Texas. Architect: CRS Inc. Photographer: Mears Photography.

122, middle: San Angelo Central High School, San Angelo, Texas. Architect: CRS Inc./Max D. Lovett. Photographer: Philip H. Hiss.

122, bottom: Elementary school, Clinton, Oklahoma. Architect: CRS Inc. Photographer: Ulric Meisel.

123, top: St. Lukes, and Texas Children's Hospital, Houston, Texas. Architect: CRS Inc. Photographer: Rob Muir.

123, middle: Midland Memorial Hospital, Midland, Texas. Architect: CRS Inc./Newhardt & Babb. Photographer: Jim Parker.

123, bottom: McKennan Hospital, Sioux Falls, South Dakota. Architect: CRS Inc./The Spitznagel Partnership, Inc. Photographer: Heidrich Blessing.

125: Seagram Building, New York. Architect: Philip C. Johnson. Photographer: Ezra Stoller.

126, top left: Baptist Church. Architect: Harry Weese. Photographer: Hedrich Blessing.

126, top right: TWA Terminal, New York. Architect: Eero Saarinen. Photographer: Balthazar Korab.

126, bottom left: Residence (built 1869), Houston, Texas. Photographer: Rick Gardner.

126, bottom right: Chaise. Designer: Charles Eames for Herman Miller Inc. Photograph: Courtesy Herman Miller Inc.

127: Adlai E. Stevenson College, University of California, Santa Cruz, California. Architect: Esherick, Homsey, Dodge, & Davis. Photographer: Ron Partridge.

128: Photographer: Balthazar Korab.

129: Church, Cedar Rapids, Iowa. Architect: Crites & McDonnell. Photographer: Julius Shulman.

130, top: German Pavilion, International Exposition 1929, Barcelona. Architect: Ludwig Mies van der Rohe. Photographer: Courtesy the Museum of Modern Art, New York.

130, bottom: Delaware Technical College, Dover Campus, Dover, Delaware. Architect: CRS Inc./Calvin P. Hamilton. Photographer: Nick Wheeler.

131: Parthenon, Athens, Greece. Architect: Ictinus. Photographer: Gordon N. Converse, *The Christian Science Monitor*.

132: Cheops, Egypt. Photograph: Courtesy Bettmann Archive.

133: Taj Mahal, India. Photograph: Courtesy Bettman Archive.

135, top: DeVry Institute, Chicago, Illinois. Architect: CRS Inc. Photographer: Orlando R. Cabanban.

135, bottom: University of Santa Clara Activities Center, Santa Clara, California. Architect: CRS Inc./Geiger-Berger Associates/Albert A. Hoover & Associates/Philip B. Welch, university architect. Photographer: Balthazar Korab.

134: Chair. Designer: Charles Eames for Herman Miller Inc. Photograph: Courtesy Herman Miller Inc.

136: Residence (built 1824–1836), near Washington On the Brazos, Texas. Architect: Restored by Thomas A. Bullock. Photograph: Courtesy Thomas A. Bullock.

137, top: Residence, Santa Monica, California. Architect: Charles Eames. Photographer: Julius Shulman.

137, bottom: Fort Wilkins (built 1842 Keweenaw Peninsula, Michigan. Photographer: Balthazar Korab.

138: William W. Wurster Hall, University of California, Berkeley, California. Architect Esherick, Homsey, Dodge, & Davis. Photograph: Courtesy Esherick, Homsey, Dodge, & Davis.

139, top: Worcester Museum Art School Worcester, Massachusetts. Architect: The Architects Collaborative, Inc. Photographer: Ezra Stoller.

139, bottom: Villita Assembly Building San Antonio, Texas. Architect: Ford, Powell, Carson Associates. Photographer Richard W. Payne.

140, top: Kahala Hilton, Honolulu, Hawaii Architect: Killingsworth, Brady & Associates. Photographer: Julius Shulman.

140, bottom: Brazosport College, Freeport, Texas. Architect: CRS Inc. Photographer: Ron Partridge.

141, top: Mississippi Research Center Jackson, Mississippi. Architect: CRS Inc. Toughstone & Biggers. Photographer Richard Payne.

141, middle: City Hall Annex, Houston Texas. Architect: CRS Inc./Bernard Johnson Engineers, Inc. Photographer: Jim Parker.

141, bottom: University of Houston Fine Arts Building, Houston, Texas. Architect CRS Inc. Photographer: Jim Parker.

142, top: Roy E. Larsen Hall, Harvard University, Cambridge, Massachusetts. Architect: CRS Inc.

142, bottom: Clarement College Science Building, Claremont, California. Architect CRS Inc./Everett Tozier. Photographer Julius Shulman.

143, top: Residence (built 1908), Victoria Texas. Photographer: Rick Gardner.

143, middle: Residence (built 1908) Pasadena, California. Architects: Greene & Greene. Photographer: Julius Shulman

143, bottom: University of Virginia, Charlottesville, Virginia. Architect: Thomas Jefferson. Photograph: Courtesy University of Virginia.

145: Hancock Center, Chicago, Illinois Architect: Skidmore, Owings, & Merrill Photographer: Hedrich Blessing.

146, top: Brazosport College, Freeport Texas. Architect: CRS Inc. Photographer Ron Partridge.

146, middle: DeVry Institute, Chicago, Illinois. Architect: CRS Inc. Photographer Jim Parker.

146, bottom: Louvre, Paris. Photograph Courtesy Bettmann Archive.

147, top: Notre Dame du Haut, Ronchamp, France. Architect: LeCorbusier Photographer: Ezra Stoller.

147, bottom: Residence, Santa Barbara California. Architect: Richard J. Neutra Photographer: Julius Shulman.

148, top: Guggenheim Museum, New York. Architect: Frank Lloyd Wright. Photographer: Balthazar Korab.

148, bottom: Residence, Chicago, Illinois. Architect: Frank Lloyd Wright. Photographer: Balthazar Korab.

149: St. Basil Church (built 16th century), Red Square, Moscow. Photographer: Gor-

Index

Page numbers in italic indicate illustrations of buildings.

Edited by Sarah Bodine and Susan Davis
Designed by James Craig
Composed in 10 point Vega Light by Publishers Graphics, Inc.
Printed and bound by Halliday Lithograph Corp.

ARCHITECTURE AND YOU

f you're looking for a book to introduce you to the pleasures of architecture; if you want to be able to enjoy buildings, just like music and art; if you want to learn how to appreciate the buildings you experience every day, as well as the ageless masterpieces, but you don't know where to begin, this is the book you've been waiting for. Here is a book that explains how to experience and appreciate the spaces and forms of architecture just as you experience a painting or a symphony. Written by practicing architects whose buildings are used by millions of people throughout the world, this down-to-earth, easy-to-read text answers the fundamental question: what is architecture and how do you perceive it? The authors communicate their love of architecture and take the mystery out of buildings so you can learn how to enjoy their magic.

Richly illustrated with 280 photographs and line drawings and summarized periodically with memorable aphorisms, the text begins by defining the term "architecture appreciation" and shows why architecture is "a personal, enjoyable, necessary experience." Then the authors cover the basics of space, form, and total-form. The "envelope" is analyzed: wall, roof, floor, window, structure, materials, connections. Style is described through such concepts as proportion, scale, and composition. Physical environment, including site and light, and psychological environment, consisting of ownership, symbolism, and color, are explored. The book shows the impact of societal needs on architecture and the concept of economy is evaluated in terms of simplicity, cost, and energy. Time quality is defined in relation to history and technology. The authors conclude by discussing the idea that "design reconciles function, form, economy, and time," and then they review all the preceding chapters in a final brief wrap-up.

This book will lead you to a new awareness of architecture and a new pleasure in your environment. You *can* enjoy buildings every day of your life.

176 pages. 8¼ x 11 (21 x 28 cm). 280 black-and-white illustrations. Glossary. Selected Reading List. Index.

William Wayne Caudill, FAIA, serves as Chairman of the Board for Caudill Rowlett Scott, Architects Planners Engineers, a firm he and John Rowlett founded in 1946. He has written or co-authored over fifty articles and reports as well as seven books. The most notable include *Architecture by Team, A Bucket of Oil: Energy Conservation through Design,* and *From Infancy to Infinity.*

William Merriweather Peña, FAIA, became Caudill Rowlett Scott's fourth principal a year after joining the firm and is now Senior Vice President and Director of the CRS Planning and Programming Services Group. He was elected a Fellow of the American Institute of Architects in 1972. Peña has authored many professional papers and the book *Problem Seeking.* He is also a well-known lecturer in the architecture profession.

Paul Kennon, AIA, is President and Chief Executive Officer of Caudill Rowlett Scott. He was senior designer with Eero Saarinen and Associates for seven years. From 1964 to 1966, Kennon lived in Santiago, Chile, as advisor for the Chilean Regional and Community Facilities Program jointly sponsored by the Ford Foundation, Rice University, Harvard University, and Caudill Rowlett Scott.

WHITNEY LIBRARY OF DESIGN
an imprint of
WATSON GUPTILL PUBLICATIONS, 1515 Broadway, New York, N.Y. 10036